PRAISE FOR SACF

In his luminous prose, Tom Steagald leads readers through the Christian year from Advent to Christ the King, weaving together fresh telling of the ancient story and poignant personal experience and observation. This little book is a find for all ready to walk through the liturgical calendar looking for new treasure hidden in the familiar.

—MICHAEL L. LINDVALL, author of *A Geography of God*

Steagald sounds the melody of God's story and then dovetails in the counterpoint of personal experience with both lines of notes hung on the staff of the Christian liturgical year. A fascinating approach.

—JAMES C. HOWELL, PhD, senior pastor, Myers Park United Methodist Church, Charlotte, North Carolina; author of twelve books, including *The Beatitudes for Today* and *Yours Are the Hands of Christ*

If we are going to follow Jesus, we will pay attention to the paths of righteousness that are set before us. Yet at times we are unclear about the traveling conditions, much less the destination. Tom Steagald has a gift for describing the spiritual journey of discipleship, helping us not only to discern where we are at each step along the way but also to envision the future with hope and confidence.

— KEN CARTER, bishop of The United Methodist Church and author of *A Way of Life in the World*

Tom Steagald packs this book with valuable resources for those beginning or already embarked on the quest to follow Jesus. He offers a delightful and imaginative retelling of key gospel stories in a setting that serves as an introduction and exploration of the liturgical calendar. The insertion of valuable theological insights and provocative questions makes it a book well worth reading.

— ROBERT O. BYRD, ThD, professor and H. F. Paschall chair of biblical studies and preaching, Belmont University

SACRED DAYS

FOLLOWING JESUS THROUGH

THE CHRISTIAN YEAR

THOMAS R. STEAGALD

UPPER
ROOM BOOKS®
NASHVILLE

SACRED DAYS: Following Jesus through the Christian Year
Copyright © 2014 by Thomas R. Steagald
All rights reserved.

Upper Room Books website: books.upperroom.org

Upper Room®, Upper Room Books®, and design logos are trademarks owned by The Upper Room®, a ministry of GBOD®, Nashville, Tennessee. All rights reserved.

Unless otherwise noted, scripture quotations are from the New Revised Standard Version Bible, copyright © 1989 National Council of the Churches of Christ in the United States of America. Used by permission. All rights reserved.

Scripture quotations noted RSV are from the Revised Standard Version of the Bible, copyright 1952 [2nd edition 1971] by the Division of Christian Education of the National Council of the Churches of Christ in the United States of America. Used by permission. All rights reserved.

Scripture quotations noted NIV are from the Holy Bible, New International Version®, NIV®. Copyright 1973, 1978, 1984, 2011 by Biblica, Inc.™ Used by permission of Zondervan. All rights reserved worldwide. www.zondervan.com.

Scripture quotations noted KJV are from the King James Version of the Holy Bible.

Scripture quotations noted AP are the author's paraphrase.

The definitions of the church seasons are taken from *Merriam-Webster's Collegiate Dictionary*, Eleventh Edition (Springfield, Massachusetts: Merriam Webster, Incorporated, 2003).

At the time of publication all website references in this book were valid. However, due to the fluid nature of the internet some addresses may have changed or the content may not longer be relevant.

Cover and interior design: Bruce Gore / gorestudio.com

LIBRARY OF CONGRESS CATALOGING-IN-PUBLICATION DATA
Steagald, Tom.
  Sacred days : following Jesus through the Christian year / by Thomas R. Steagald.
    pages cm
  Includes bibliographical references.
  ISBN 978-0-8358-1381-5 (print)—ISBN 978-0-8358-1382-2 (mobi)—ISBN 978-0-8358-1383-9 (epub)
  1. Church year—Miscellanea. I. Title.
  BV30.S66 2015
  242'.3—dc23   2014030545

Printed in the United States of America

For the past ministers, former and current members
of Hawthorne Lane United Methodist Church,
Charlotte, North Carolina, on the occasion
of their Centennial of worship, ministry, and service;

and for Carrie Smith Wright and Sarah Watkins Davis, sisters,
colleagues and friends;

and for Carolyn, Dawn, Jim, Allan, and Akram,
co-laborers in the work.

∞

*"Thine they were, and thou gavest them to me,
and they have kept thy word."*
—John 17:6, RSV

The liturgical calendar as a whole exists in large part to remind us that Christ has sanctified all of time, bringing the whole of our experience into the orbit of resurrection. What we deem ordinary, God has transformed into the extraordinary by the power of divine grace.

—Laurence Hull Stookey
Calendar: Christ's Time for the Church

CONTENTS

ACKNOWLEDGMENTS

What does anyone who speaks of you really say? Yet woe betide those who fail to speak while the chatterboxes go on saying nothing.
—SAINT AUGUSTINE, *The Confessions*, Book 1, paragraph 4

Saint Augustine, bishop of Hippo and Doctor of the Church, long ago prayed that prayer. All these centuries later I find deep resonance in his confession; he states far better my ambivalence as I preface this, yet another book on Jesus.

I know better than anyone else that I have said nothing new. What *new*, really, is there to say? And how dare I? I am no scholar or wise man. My elders and betters have more eloquently told many of these same stories, have offered many of these same insights, have asked and even answered many of these same questions. Perhaps I should have stayed my hand and kept my heart and mouth shut.

But I also know the demand of the subject. Like prophets, like apostles and martyrs, like saints both windowed and nameless, like my professors and pastors and Sunday school teachers—and like my own father not least—I know the burning that comes with not speaking. I know the fire in the bones that compels testimony.

So within the limits set by my experience and awareness, I have tried to muster the best words I could to tell the "old, old story" in hopes that it will come to life again in the hearing of the reader. I know that such a result is properly the work of the Holy Spirit; I only hope, following the recent counsel of Amy-Jill Levine, I have given the Holy Spirit something to work with.

Phillips Brooks defined preaching as "truth through personality." This definition is too pristine by half, but in any case it is more or less what happens Sunday by Sunday. Truth, or something akin to it, is refracted through the experiences and disposition of the preacher so as to be fleshed out in words and gesture. It is a solitary task in many ways, even a lonely one, preparing this most public expression of one's call to ministry. I'm thankful that preaching is done "in the midst," in a congregation that by grace can turn the loneliness into community and the preaching itself into dialogue.

Writing too may share with preaching both the burden of solitude and the (potential) joy of community. I am so thankful to have been blessed to live and work—not geographically but relationally—among a group of interested others who have taken my reflections and introspections as cues for genuine conversation.

INTRODUCTION

Jesus Calls, Disciples Follow

Wherever He leads, I'll go.
—B. B. McKinney

Jesus comes to the shore of the Sea of Galilee, as perhaps he's come many times before. This time he stops near the two fishermen Simon and Andrew who are casting their nets into the shallow waters. "Follow me," he says. Maybe they know him—or maybe not. Either way, the two men drop their nets, wade out of the shallows, and follow him.

A little farther up the shore Jesus stops near a boat. It belongs to old Zebedee, but soon it will belong to Zebedee's two sons when his own fishing days are over. He will give them the boat and the business, the hired hands and his private map of all the best fishing spots. He will settle down to enjoy his retirement, his grandchildren. But on this day Jesus stops at Zebedee's boat. Two other men pause with Jesus, huddling a ways behind, former fishermen themselves. Jesus calls to Zebedee's sons, James and John, much the same way he called to Simon and Andrew, and the old man can only watch as in a heartbeat all his plans change.

Did Jesus call anyone else that day? Any of the servants or even old Zebedee himself? We don't know. But Jesus does call James and John who up and leave their father and the boat and the nets and the servants. They fall in with Simon and Andrew, following after Jesus. Does Zebedee bless them as they go or curse them, his heart, like his imagined future, breaking as a wave on the shore? Does he have the first idea what his sons are doing? No more than they, I suppose, but we can only speculate. All we know for sure is that now five sets of footprints track the sand where there had been only one.

Frame the moment, the picture: Jesus comes to the fishermen where they are and calls to them. They answer, the first of many men and women who do, and off they go. They go because Jesus called. They walk with him *away* from the Sea of Galilee because he came *to* the Sea of Galilee seeking disciples. The steps they take are a response of faith; his are the initiative of grace. Jesus calls. Disciples follow.

Every disciple's journey begins with answering Jesus, and answering Jesus always means following him step by step wherever he leads. While those first disciples did not know where that might be, what those new places and situations might demand, they worked hard to keep pace.

∞

"Follow me" is never an easy command to obey, for discipleship often means going with Jesus from place to place. He does not stay long anywhere but is always moving on to the next town, the next synagogue, the next need. Discipleship is harder yet on the ears and the head and hardest of all on the heart, whose highways are built over mountainous rationalizations, gouged deep by storms of selfishness and self-doubt.

But "make straight in the desert a highway for our God" (40:4), the prophet Isaiah cries, and we believe he means in the world and also in us. By God's own word all the mountains will be flattened and the valleys filled up—all the rough places smoothed—that the Lord might come to us and we in turn might follow him as on level ground. Jesus seeks to enlist us in God's work in the world, calls us to learn God's ways and God's will, and trains us for service as God's emissaries.

I use the Christian year (the Temporal Cycle, as it is sometimes called) as a map. The seasons of the Christian year—from Advent through the Reign of Christ—constitute the church's traditional telling of the story of Jesus' life and also suggest an implicit itinerary for our journey with him. As we recount Jesus' movements, season to season, we will affirm certain aspects of his life and work. Those affirmations will prompt the confession that because we often remain self-focused as individuals and as a church, we often fail to go where Jesus goes, to do what Jesus does. But with confession comes the opportunity for repentance and renewed dedication to go wherever Jesus leads.

But why use the Christian year as a map? Week by week, year by year, a patterned reading of the Gospels recounts both Jesus' life and his claim on the disciples who chose to follow him. The "seasons" of his life proclaim that Jesus is the Light of the World (Advent), born both King of the Jews (Christmas) and Savior of the world (Epiphany). His saving work will occasion resistance and suffering (Lent) and lead eventually to his death (Holy Week and Good Friday). But death is not the last word (Easter Day), and both in his person and in the sending of the Holy Spirit, Jesus gives life, memory, and power to his disciples (Easter season and Pentecost).

Many branches of the Christian family worship according to this seasonal rhythm, not only to herald those truths but also to confess that our concerns are narrower than our summons—that we remain in the dark still, that we are parochial in our perspective, loathe to suffer, and minimalist in our understanding of Resurrection and Spirit. The value of the Christian year, then, is both pastoral and practical, both historic and contemporary.

Observing the Temporal Cycle involves a prophetic aspect as well; part of our fallen nature entails that we pick and choose what we like best about Jesus and the Gospels and ignore or discount the rest. As Lauren Winner has noted, many godly and well-meaning people have unwittingly taught recent generations of believers to read the Bible only in snippets, without a sense of the great narrative sweep of scripture or our own part in the Story.[1] Contemporary preaching has also deepened the crisis. In many of our congregations we hear mostly "how-to" sermons, often founded on small portions of scripture and forced into mechanistic formulas to offer easy political, moral, or even financial lessons.

Recalling the fuller life and ministry of Jesus by means of the Christian year helps us avoid the kind of fragmentation and gnostic disembodiment that can occur when we recall only our favorite stories or read our three-minute devotionals. The Temporal Cycle reiterates it all again year after year, the whole life and ministry of Jesus; his coming and call in all its fullness, which is our best guide to discipleship.

By means of midrash—biblical and theological reflections—but with a bit of memoir too, I will tell the Story. Along the way, I hope readers will gain new insights for reading the texts as well as new ways to navigate the distance from head to heart and to live their faith more authentically.

Advent [Middle English, from Medieval Latin *adventus*, from Latin, arrival, from *advenire*] **1:** the period beginning four Sundays before Christmas and observed by some Christians as a season of prayer and fasting **2a:** the coming of Christ at the Incarnation

Christmas

Epiphany

Lent

Holy Week

Easter

Pentecost

Trinity

Ordinary Time

Reign of Christ

I

Promises in the Dark

ADVENT

Does anyone believe the galaxies exist to add splendor to the night sky over Bethlehem?

—ANNIE DILLARD

In the beginning, when God created the heavens and the earth, there was nothing but darkness and a formless void. God hovered over the face of the deep, silenced the howl of confusion, filled the emptiness with divine will and word. "Let there be light," God said, and there was light. Not many days later, much more existed: land and sea and life enough to fill them both. The darkness remained a part of things but confined and partitioned—the dusk itself serving as a kind of overture for the dawn.

At week's end God kneels in the good garden, scoops damp earth into hands and works it, molds and shapes something quite unlike anything yet made. God then breathes into *'adam* God's own misty breath, and the dirt comes alive with the life of God.

The Man, God's fingerprints all over him, coughs and arises, squints into his first awareness of the Good Garden, awakens to his first dim notions of the Good Gardener. Soon comes Woman and the prospect of offspring—all of it so very good, the heavens and the earth, that God rests.

And then all hell breaks loose. The darkness whelms its partition, surges over into every place and thing, every thought and motive. Night now signals the end, not the beginning. When the Man and the Woman break the lone command God has given them, the sun dims and so does the vision of the Man and Woman. Darker still grows the countenance of their firstborn against his younger brother and soon not only the children of the earth but even the earth itself languishes and mourns. The only clear light radiates from the angel's flaming sword. Thorns choke the flowers and fields.

The children of the earth were fruitful but withered, almost beyond recognition. They multiplied but were diminished, weakened, no longer able to subdue the earth or even enjoy it completely. Instead, they used the earth, were punished by it, and tilled it in uneasy truce. The Good Garden became a bad and lonely place as the Man, the Woman, and all their unfortunate offspring nearly forgot the intimacy for which they were created and instead spent their days isolated, segregated, fearful. The children of the earth rebelled against their Maker, tried to deny both God's image and God's word. They ignored God's fingerprints on them, spurned God's counsel, and maintained that both were fictions forced on the naive.

In most of our generation the rebellion continues unabated, either in active disobedience or thoughtless disregard. Like the Man and the Woman before us, we find ourselves in terrified exile from we are not sure what. Squinting, not for the splendor of the light anymore but on account of blindness, we, like all the descendants of the Man and the Woman, can only *almost* see the place we really belong. We carry in our collective awareness a hazy sense of what should be and a clear conviction that current experience is not it. Our senses grow increasingly numb to true beauty, impatient with "received" wisdom, as ignorance holds our thoughts captive.

The earth and its children still languish and mourn. That is the hard, bad news.

It would have been no surprise if God had chosen to blot out the world, to start over from scratch. But the good, true news is that God has never been able to brush us off, not entirely. Even the Flood was not water enough to get us off God's hands.

God made the world and gave it to us as a gift. We broke it quickly and completely, but God determined to fix what was broken—both the world and us. The Good Gardener chose a man and his family—Noah and his heirs—to be the seeds of a new crop.

God delivered and constituted a people, Israel; sent laws and rituals, priests, prophets, and kings, so that through them light might again shine in the world's darkness like new day. It was a re-creation, that the world itself might be blessed, the earth gradually a garden once more. But the many laws were disobeyed as quickly as Eden's, and the people were soon in disarray. Their kings and priests and prophets proved as hard-hearted as the dry earth where the holy[1] people lived, as prickly as the thorns and broken as the world they were sent to redeem. As the fields grew more barren, the darkness grew deeper.

∞

On the first Sunday of Advent I invite the children of the congregation down to the front of the sanctuary for the children's sermon, a liturgically suspect but customary element of morning worship. When they arrive, I hold in my hand a butane lighter. Silently, once, twice, three times I pull the trigger. Blue and orange flame leaps from the tip. The kids say nothing, transfixed by the sight of the flame.

"What have I just done?" I ask them. Little hands shoot into the air, polite eagerness. "You are making fire," one says. "That's what we use to light the altar candles," notes another. "You're playing a game!" states an older child.

"It is fun," I reply, "but it is not a game. Not really. I've said a prayer." All look puzzled. "A *prayer?*" says one incredulously.

"Absolutely," I respond. "When we light the candles on our altar or pull the trigger on the lighter or even strike a match, it is like a prayer. We are confessing—do you know that word? *Confessing? Confession?* We are admitting, confessing, that we are in the dark, like when you are in your house and there is a storm, thunder and lightning. The lights go out, and you feel afraid. When it is really dark, all of us get scared. We don't know if we are alone or if someone is with us. What we all wish is that the lights would come back on.

"Sometimes we use the words *in the dark* to mean that we don't understand why things happen the way they do. We don't know why other people are the way they are; we don't even always know why we are like we are.

"We light the candle," I say, "and it is like asking God to send us more light." And we believe that somehow and some way God always answers that prayer.

∞

Seven hundred years before the time of Jesus, the prophet Isaiah saw a vision, a vision we recall each Advent season:

> A shoot shall come out from the stump of Jesse,
>   and a branch shall grow out of his roots,
> The spirit of the LORD shall rest on him (Isa. 11:1-2).

Isaiah offers a two-sided vision: a vision both of judgment and of grace. God is coming and will soon send a light so bright as to blind eyes too comfortable in the dark, a lamp that will illumine minds discontent in the long, deep shadows. God is coming: The promise and prospect bring both judgment and mercy. Isaiah sees both at once, and that is precisely why we remember his prophecies each Advent season.

Like Isaiah's vision, the season of Advent—beginning the fourth Sunday before Christmas Day and ending Christmas Eve—proclaims both grace and judgment, mercy and indictment. It is grace, a joy and a celebration, that Jesus is coming to save us. God loves the world so much that God sends the Son, that whoever believes in him should not die but live forever. But Jesus' coming bears judgment too. It confirms the indictment that the world is indeed perishing, and Jesus must come lest we drown in the darkness. We stand amazed at Jesus' nearness, yet terrified to know that his presence portends not only life but also death—and not only for him. All the instruments and idols and powers of darkness die with him, the idolatries and darkness in ourselves as well, that light once again may shine forth as on the world's first day.

In his vision, Isaiah foretells the end of old things and the beginning of new things, the death of what had seemed immortal—the kingdom of Israel and the throne of David—and the resurrection of what, long years after the coming destruction of the Davidic rule, would have seemed to be irretrievably lost.

But Isaiah sees something more: God's preparation of an otherwise unimaginable redemption on the far side of the doom. After all is reduced to rubble and ash, while the cities still smolder and all of Israel's kings are either dead or gone, Isaiah sees the spirit of God moving across the face of the dark destruction, brooding over the ruined valleys and hills, caressing and coaxing and watering that dry stump of Jesse till a shoot comes forth, a surprising sprig from dead roots. The prophet proclaims the coming of a king from the withered loins of David's long-dead father, announces the arrival of a son and wise ruler who will put matters right again, who will build up the ancient ruins and strengthen the weak knees. On this Coming One the Spirit of the Lord will rest, giving him the gifts of wisdom and understanding and might, knowledge and compassion and fear of the Lord. Isaiah describes him this way:

> He shall not judge by mere appearances
>> nor decide under the influence of spin,
> but with righteousness he will vindicate the oppressed
>> and advocate with equity for the meek of the earth.
> His word will reorder the world
>> and his life-giving breath will be the death of oppressors. (Isa. 11:1-4, AP)

For far too long there has been no justice, no truth, no peace. But Isaiah declares that a new ruler is coming.

Seven centuries before the angel appears to a young woman of Nazareth, Isaiah sees the coming of One who for his own time, for his own people and circumstance, will be Emmanuel. Much, much later, after the virgin from Nazareth has conceived and given birth to a son, those who love him, follow him, and preach his message will read Isaiah's prophecy and recognize the face and work of their friend Jesus. In *him* judgment and mercy meet, "righteousness and peace will kiss" (Ps. 85:10), and the power of the Holy Spirit gives birth to a new people.

∞

The promise of Advent is the wonderful, horrible promise of a new king, a new thing, a new way, and a new One sent to set things right. Some can smell the aroma of God's imminent justice like coming rain. Others smell only smoke. Many sense nothing at all, and not everyone will welcome God's reign when it arrives at last.

But the promise of Advent reminds us that God is coming nonetheless, sending the heart of God's own heart to be what others were not so that God's children might not be alone, the very light of God in the darkness so that hearts and minds might be illumined, the very healing of God so that the earth itself and all its people might be whole.

$$\infty$$

We embrace the darkness, but God knows we can no longer see, at least not clearly. We have all but forgotten home; we search for that which we can no longer name. But in compassion God sends us a Shepherd, a Guide and Guardian. We are wounded, deny it as we will, and life is pouring out of us. We finger the emptiness as we would a scar, bandage it with burlap, palliate it with various poison elixirs. We love that which will kill us; we hate that which may heal us. We look for security, for comfort, in all the wrong places—such is our madness, the ancient chaos, the dark night of our soul's world. Into that very darkness God comes; God ever comes. God does not abandon us to our own self-destruction but sends light, speaks promise, and gives new life.

Advent provides the dark background to every portrait of Jesus. It confesses our present plight and proclaims the coming light. It does not engage in denial or optimism, escapism or opiates. Advent is, instead, the most "protestant" of seasons, protesting and militating for joy in spite of the grim sadness in us and in the world. It avows the deep brokenness of all things, the ruin of the world and its children, and hails the healing of both. Advent admits to our fears and failure and invokes a hope to usurp and supplant them. It proclaims a coming redemption that, though we cannot see it whole, is even now on its way.

We confess we are in the dark. That is our side of the conversation in Advent. "Mercy and grace," God says yet again. "Peace and love." These promises in the dark, signature gifts, offer illumination and hope for every lightless place. God, acknowledging that we are dust, stoops once again to cradle us, to cradle grace for us, to breathe into us that living breath.

Having loved us in the beginning, God will love us to the end. And endlessly in between, in every moment and maze, God calls to us, sings to us, invites us back into Eden, back into the very intimacies with God and each other for which we were made. God waits, looks, hopes, and desires that all God's children return home to food and song and reunion. Though we pretend to be content in the pigsty of our rebellions, below our protestations we long for home as God's patient heart beats a cadence for our return. God comes to us that we might come back to God. The Transcendent comes near to us in love. It is a long, hard journey on both ends, whether God's trek to us or ours to God.

∞

Many years ago now, during a dark and extremely scary time in my life, when tears were my food both day and night, I found myself working second shift for minimum wage at a bookstore in Atlanta. I was the assistant manager, which meant I was the one to get in trouble if the cash drawer was short, the one who had to close and lock the doors.

As luck would have it—I guess it was luck—the sections of the store that fell under my primary responsibility were "Religion" (comprised of Christianity, Judaica, world religions, the occult) and "Recovery." Many, many nights I saw people come into the store and, turning neither to the right nor to the left, head straight toward the big sign hanging from the ceiling that said "Self-Help," our best-selling section.

One December night I saw a young woman standing in the aisle, her heavy coat and scarf unable to hide the shaking of her shoulders as she quietly sobbed. I felt worried about her at once, my pastor's heart wanting to lend a pastor's ear and maybe a pastor's hand to her, whatever the trouble. I approached her, at first as if to offer customer service: "Can I help you find something?"

The woman did not look up at first but said in a quavering voice, "I wish you could. I need to find *something*."

"You need help then," I said after a moment.

Her throat clutched. "Yeah, I do. I need help."

"So do I," I said. "So do we all, and the poor dark world besides." At that moment, she turned and looked at me. I could see her puffy eyes and blotchy skin. She was a mess and not just because her mascara wasn't waterproof. For the briefest of moments, I moved from being the assistant manager to being her impromptu counselor. I pointed up to the big sign above us and whispered, "But the help we need, my friend, is beyond the self to provide."

I left the young woman to assist another customer. When I looked back, she was gone. I sometimes wonder what happened to her. One part of me thinks she is still there, our lady of perpetual desperation, still crying, still scanning the latest batch of self-help titles by the latest gaggle of self-help gurus, her shoulders still shaking and her makeup still streaked because there is no help there, no real healing, no lasting hope. She represents a study in futility because she believes she has to help herself, make whatever little good might happen happen, build her best life now because God—if there is a God—helps only those who help themselves.

But another part of me thinks she took that little piece of advice, followed those simple directions, took a step toward Jesus and the church, and there found what she could not find before: something bigger and better and beyond herself, a sprig growing from dry wood, a Savior who knows who we are and what we need and how to give it to us. In him we find ways to understand the times, the moments, and the meanings of our lives—the first inklings of healing.

I pray that into the rough timbers of her life and circumstances, holiness was born that night, that Christ's presence came as light in her darkness. That likewise into our lives and the world's life, Christ may come.

Even so, come quickly, Lord Jesus.

Affirmation: Creation is good but broken.

Confession: We too are broken.

Discipleship Task: To see the world and ourselves realistically and to wait, praying for the healing Jesus alone can bring.

Advent

Christmas [Middle English *Christemasse*, from Old English *Cristes masse*, literally, Christ's mass] **1:** a Christian feast on December 25 or among some Eastern Orthodox Christians on January 7 that commemorates the birth of Christ and is usually observed as a legal holiday

    Epiphany

    Lent

    Holy Week

    Easter

    Pentecost

    Trinity

    Ordinary Time

    Reign of Christ

2

God with Us

CHRISTMAS

In Jesus' birth . . . Christians believe two wonderful things happen. First, God takes the human life of Jesus into God's own eternal life, and in so doing, Jesus' people (the Jews), species (the human race), and history (the history of our whole planet and our whole universe) enter into—are taken up into—God's own life. . . . Second, as humanity (and all creation) enters into God through Jesus, God also enters Jesus' people, species, and history. And by entering all creation through Jesus, God's heart is forever bound to it in solidarity, faithfulness, loyalty, and commitment. God will never give up until all creation is healed. . . . Jesus saves by coming, by being born.

—BRIAN MCLAREN

Zechariah, the old and wizened husband of childless Elizabeth, the elder relative of unmarried Mary, is a priest, a righteous man and full of the Holy Spirit, as is his wife. But his flesh is as dry as a wood plank. One day while serving in the Temple, perhaps for the first and only time in his long, priestly life, the angel Gabriel visits Zechariah and tells him that he and Elizabeth are going to be parents.

Startled, Zechariah questions the angel, "How can this be when I am ancient? Elizabeth and I have already forgotten the old tricks; how can we learn any new ones?" (Luke 1:6, AP).

Zechariah's response to the news annoys Gabriel and rightly so. After all, this is no ordinary announcement and Gabriel no ordinary messenger. Besides, as a priest Zechariah would surely have remembered Israel's stories, how Sarah, Rachel, and Hannah, though childless, conceived in their old age because with God nothing is impossible. The Temple in which Zechariah stands bears witness through its stones and songs, its sacrifices and stories, that God comes when and how God wills.

And so Gabriel summarily mutes Zechariah for his impudence. The old priest will remain silent for the next nine months with his faithless foot in his mouth. But his punishment will prove a blessing. He can ponder his next words carefully, choose them a bit more wisely. Sure enough, when he does speak again, his words issue in the praise of God. Zechariah finally has it right.

We ourselves might do well with a season of silence, if only because our busyness with work and making our way in the world precludes our hearing the heavenly word if it comes. "Do not be afraid," perhaps, or "Your prayer has been heard." We experience so much movement in our world and in our lives that without stilling ourselves and taking time to listen, we will never hear the still small voice of God.

If Gabriel silences the old priest because he hears God's promises and does not trust them, we may need silencing *to* hear them.

∞

In the sixth month of Zechariah's silence and Elizabeth's pregnancy, a virgin named Mary espoused to a tradesman named Joseph, living in Nazareth, has a similar visitation. Gabriel appears to her and announces that she will conceive and bear a son—the same message that Gabriel had delivered to Zechariah. But if his incredulity was surprising, hers is not.

"How can this be, since I am a virgin?" (Luke 1:34).

This time Gabriel answers gently: "The Holy Spirit will come upon you, will overshadow you, will conceive holiness in you, and you shall bear in your womb and deliver to this earth a savior" (Luke 1:35, AP). From Gabriel's lips to Mary's ear. Her response arises from deep within her: "Let it be with me according to your word" (Luke 1:38). By God's own initiative the Word is made with Mary's flesh. Mary is but the first of the *theotokoi*.[1] She cradles the Christ in her womb. But all those who do the will of God and answer the call to discipleship are not only Jesus' friends and followers, his brothers and sisters, but also his *mother*. (See Mark 3:35.) Those who hear God's command and do it, who "bring good news to the poor, . . . proclaim release to the captives and recovery of sight to the blind, . . . let the oppressed go free, [and] . . . proclaim the year of the Lord's favor" (Luke 4:18-19)—all of them gestate God's will, give birth to God's Word and purposes in the world. The Holy Spirit comes, overshadows, and holiness is born. Mary births Jesus once; his disciples give birth to him over and over and over again.

Gabriel does not silence Mary as he did Zechariah but instead gives her voice to sing a song of faith—the Magnificat—which she sings a short time later in the home of her relative Elizabeth:

My soul magnifies the Lord,
and my spirit rejoices in God my Savior,
for he has looked with favor on the lowliness of his servant.
Surely, from now on all generations will call me blessed;
for the Mighty One has done great things for me,
and holy is his name. (Luke 1:46-49)

Compare the two moments: Gabriel's visit to the old priest and then to the young virgin six months later. The stories are so alike, yet so very different. Mary (and Elizabeth) sing praise to God earlier and more faithfully. Zechariah eventually does as well but only after many silent nights.

When Mary visits Elizabeth, the women do all the talking. They rejoice in God's work in the world through their children. Soon the "haves" will be the "have-nots." The "have-nots" will possess it all—the favor and blessing and mercy of God. The swollen, prideful kings will soon wither, humiliated. The powerful who have gained wealth at the expense of the poor will trade places with the outcast and the downtrodden. The outcasts will revel in a prosperity of God's own making.

Mary and Elizabeth know, *know*, that their sons are swords in the hands of God, cutting and cleaving. Soon the lowly will lift their voices in praise and thanksgiving, just as this barren old woman and her young virgin cousin do: talking and singing, offering God and each other mystified thanks and adulation.

The highest praise is not imitation but amazed interrogation.

"Why has this happened to me," Elizabeth asks in wonder, "that the mother of my Lord comes to me?" (Luke 1:43).

"How can this be," the blessed virgin Mary asks innocently, "that the mighty arm of God has been revealed and it is the arm of a newborn? That all the purposes and power of God are enfleshed in my flesh, gestating in the darkness of my womb?" (Luke 1:51-55, AP).

"How can this be?" Surely Joseph asks it too, as dumbfounded as Zechariah when he asked the question of Gabriel. Joseph asks the question of Mary and God, whether in rage or despair or both.

∞

We do not know much about Joseph and are the poorer for it. Apocryphal stories[2] about him reveal that he was an old man, over ninety, when he was chosen by lot to be the guardian as much as the husband of Mary.

Mary's mother, Anna, had conceived Mary in her old age and dedicated her daughter to God's service. Anna brought Mary to the Temple when Mary was twelve, at about the same time Joseph—a priest and father of six grown children—was left a widower at age eighty-nine. Two years later, when Mary was fourteen, the priests drew straws to see who would serve as caretaker for Mary, and Joseph found himself married to the young virgin. He was mostly beyond suspicion when her pregnancy was at last revealed and soon he moved his second family to Nazareth where he lived another twenty years, dying at the age of 111.

To some early believers, this age disparity seemed a nice if indirect proof not only of Jesus' virginal conception but also of Mary's perpetual virginity.[3] It also helps explain why we never again hear of Joseph after the trip to the Temple when Jesus is twelve and Joseph is, by my calculations, 103.

I don't believe much of that though. I am more inclined to think of Mary and Joseph's relationship as typical, their love genuine, their plans more or less normal, and their future hopeful (if not terribly promising, what with Joseph a carpenter in a rocky land in the midst of Roman occupation). But every couple in young love sees the future as a cup brimming with promise, and the two must have talked about the home they planned to make, the draperies, and the dishes. Surely they talk about children too, how many they hope to have and when. Everything, it seems, is going along as planned when . . .

"Joseph," Mary says quietly, "I am going to have a baby."

How Joseph has wanted to hear those words—but not now, not like this. And now, whenever he hears them again, they will be a knife to his heart. If Joseph is human, even if he believes, he also doubts. Even if he hopes, he also despairs—for many reasons, not least that Mary, his wife, is not carrying *his* child.

Joseph is afraid too. Afraid that what Mary tells him is not true and perhaps even more afraid that it is. Angry and scared, happy and sad, ready to put her away and eager to keep her close, Joseph tries to hold on. Finally he decides to divorce her, cancel their agreement—but quietly, mercifully. He does not want a scandal for her, does not want her accused of adultery and banished, or worse. Only then, *after* his gracious decision, does Joseph receive an angelic visitation of his own, his own divine confirmation that all is true. "Let it be to *me* according to your will," he may have prayed.

Does he believe it, what Mary has told him? Does he trust the angel, or that it was an angel at all, and not his own wishful dreaming. Do we believe because of our dreams or dream because of our beliefs? The poet W. H. Auden maintains that Joseph was the first Christian: He decided to believe the news of the Incarnation and order his life accordingly, all without proof. He lived *as if* it was true, that his faith would become sight, his hope knowledge—the first of many to do so.[4]

The trajectory of discipleship seems to be this: We live faithfully until by grace we have faith. We hear the call, the announcement, the summons. God's call moves us one way or the other, shuffles our feet or opens our hands. By grace, that call softens our heart (its final destination), and then we live faithfully because we have faith.

We travel on our way, living our lives *as if*, living in light of what ought to be true, even though we cannot be absolutely sure on this side of death that it is. We trace our steps by the hope of something beyond the path we see and the directions we hear, acknowledging if we dare that we may be fools to do so. Somehow we find the strength to keep answering, to keep moving, to keep making space for God to appear. We set our sights by what "cannot be seen," as Paul fashioned it, for "what can be seen is temporary, but what cannot be seen is eternal" (2 Cor. 4:18). We keep going, believing and not, hoping and despairing, trusting that what we have heard—the call to faithfulness—is the truest of all true things, the truth beneath all appearance.

And so the Holy Family—Mary, Joseph, and the unborn Savior—make their uncomfortable way, each of them bearing a heavy burden and all of them together a parable of our own pilgrim journeys until the Son of God be revealed at last. That day is near. God's will will be done. Redemption draws nigh; but until it arrives, there is night.

In those days Caesar said that everyone had to travel to his or her ancestral home to be counted and taxed. Even pregnant young women and perplexed young men had to hit the road. It is a long way from Nazareth to Bethlehem. A long way from God's heart to Mary's womb. A long way from heaven to earth.

Mary and Joseph arrive in Bethlehem, she on a donkey and Jesus in her womb. Joseph leads them both, being led himself. Each of them, in his or her own way, is in the dark about what lies ahead. There is no room for them in the town's inns. We do not know where the Holy Family found shelter—a cave, perhaps. So some traditions say . . . a makeshift stable. We do not know exactly when Jesus was born. It is always so, always as mysterious as it is promised and experienced. That holy night, whenever and wherever it was, whether they are ready for all of it or for any of it, the baby is born. And Joseph names him Jesus.

Jesus. A name that translates, "Lord, save us." When Joseph names the baby Jesus, he utters a prayer for himself and the world. Mary's is the first womb, but the world itself, all its times and peoples, is where God will swaddle the Divine. Jesus is born in the cave outside Bethlehem for the sake of all who walk or sleep or are buried in the darkness. God so loves the world, but we sometimes forget.

Christmas, as we often observe it, blinds us to anything but Christmas itself. Its properties are those of an icon—a window opened to grant our prayers access to God. By grace God grants us, if we will, to see through the celebration itself to the Creator's love of creation. "Glory to God in the highest heaven, and on earth peace" (Luke 2:14) is not a clichéd refrain for the children's angel chorus on pageant night but the full measure of God's will for the world and its children. Jesus, born to save the world, comes as healer for all God's wounded children.

∽

Each year on December 21, still on Advent's dark highway but almost in sight of Bethlehem's lights, I schedule a service called "The Longest Night." The service, following the writings of Ann Weems, is for "those who weep and those who weep with those who weep."[5] The sanctuary lights are dim, the room illumined mostly by candles. The candles provide barely enough light to read the dark scriptures, sing the bleak midwinter hymns, and remember all those for whom the Christmas season is unsparing and brutal. Deep grief surfaces from among some of the worshipers because of various separations from loved ones. One year a woman stood to tell us in a cracking voice of her son who was addicted to so many things and so very lost. She told us how she and her husband had lived with the shame of their son's plight, the guilt that they had done something wrong, and how the the burden of his brokenness crushed them. The son's situation strained their marriage. They had little to say to each other or anyone else, so withered were their spirits, each of them defending what they needed to confess, hiding what they needed to share, grieving and angry in their own way, and unable to find a place or way to lay any of it down. Until that night. She offered her wounded heart to Jesus as she and her husband went to the altar to light a candle for their son, for his ex-wife and children—a prayer for all of them.

Suddenly, the room moved. Everyone attending the service stood and moved to the front to join them, to touch them, to hug and cry with them, to tell them of their love. On the heels of lonely confession came intimacy, as in our sanctuary, dark as the Bethlehem cave, there came light.

We gather each year to pray, to leave our fears and shame at the twinkling altar, hoping against hope that the Light shining in darkness will shine into our hearts and lives and the world as well. We sing:

O little town of Bethlehem, how still we see thee lie;
above thy deep and dreamless sleep the silent stars go by.
Yet in thy dark streets shineth the everlasting light;
the hopes and fears of all the years are met in thee tonight.
For Christ is born of Mary, . . .

Christ is born of Mary. The darkness of Mary's womb cradled the Savior, a Light to all people. The dark road to Bethlehem, a parable of our own dark roads, found its way. The overcrowded town, itself a parable of our overcrowded lives, hosted the baby.

Advent is not just the story of Mary's pregnancy but also of Elizabeth's and indeed the world's. The whole creation groans as if in labor pains until all that God has promised is delivered. Until then, we make our uncomfortable way forward, remembering the stories and letting what we hear find its way to our heart. Let it be to all of us according to your word, whatever that word may be. We hope and despair by turns that new life is possible on the other side of the darkness and pain, but we proclaim that God's promise is good, that the Promised One is coming.

But "can anything good come out of Nazareth?" (John 1:46). How indeed can anything good come *to* Nazareth or *to* Bethlehem, to the world or even to our own lives? The answer, which forms the root of the Story, is at once long familiar, while remaining a surprise: grace, inestimable mercy, self-prompted divine initiative.

God determined to intervene in our helplessness, to stab the darkness, to come to our aid. Though King of the universe, God will not be separated from God's unfortunate people. Though high and lifted up, God will not remain impassive to the weary misery of the world's children. Having heard their cries, the Lord condescends, self-empties, fills the valleys, and levels the mountains with a cross. God proved the divine power by humility, suffering, and service. As it was in the beginning, is now, and ever shall be: God with us; Jesus is born.

∞

Someone fashioned Bethlehem's manger, rough and splintery and uneven as its boards may have been. The laborer did not know the full meaning of his work, what grace the manger would hold. He opened a crack, shaped a place, divided the air, and made a space so that a living thing of its own accord could draw near, whether sheep or cows, shepherds or wise men, even the Lamb who is the Christ.

The Bethlehem worker made a trough, but God cribbed salvation within. Still, Jesus could not have been swaddled precisely *there* had the laborer not sawed and hammered, bashed his thumbs, to make something to hold *something.*

We sometimes see light in the cracks of our lives. God's light seeps through our broken places. Our prayers may open a space for God to come, but it is God who decides *to* come, to bring holiness to us, to note our hammering attentions and answer our rasping saws.

So we keep at it: saying our prayers, entering a cave should God decide to visit. We garner no guarantee, of course. The prayer itself may prove the answer to our praying; our work does not guarantee the arrival of righteousness. God is not on call. God, rather, does the calling and shows up where and when God chooses.

Still, what choice do we have? We do as we have been instructed. We pray. We clothe the naked. We visit the prisons or feed the hungry, and who knows? Perhaps one Christmas Eve as we stand in the local soup kitchen ladling the steaming broth, the eyes of a stranger will look up to us, and, as if through a plume of incense, we will see God come as one of the least of these.

Through the dark and broken places—that is where the light most often seeps. A Bethlehem cave, a hole in the hillside, an emptiness more than a presence, a rough-hewn manger, our rough-and-tumble lives and world, the house of our souls, as Augustine rightly saw, is no more than clapboard and emptiness. Our world is a hovel, one way or the other, but God comes. Bidden or unbidden, *vocare atque non vocare*—in spite of all, holiness gets born.

Somewhere. Sometime. Then in Bethlehem, now among us.

Not always where we would think to look for it, but always where we will find it if we have the eyes to see.

When we least expect it.

When we most need it.

Sometimes in the mangers we have readied for him, and sometimes in a space we have built for something else entirely.

God's grace, our work: Both play a part, but the phrases are not equally weighted. The latter depends wholly on the first, is the gist of our hopes and our prayers. We do our work, yes, but all the work we do offers barest preparation. Holiness appears of its own accord.

Jesus arrives when the days are "accomplished" (Luke 2:6, KJV). When the time is right, he comes. His holiness sanctifies the manger of our lives; his birth fills the dark caves of our world with light. Joy to the *world*. The Lord is come.

But not everyone seems happy about it.

∞

On December 26, the second day of Christmas, when our true love would give us what in Jesus' day was a Temple sacrifice especially prescribed for the poor—two turtledoves—we remember and celebrate the martyrdom and sacrifice of Stephen. The Feast of Stephen, known to many only through the carol "Good King Wenceslas," commemorates a solemn moment in the church year. In it we recall the life and faithful death of the first person to die for *being* a disciple. It serves as a stark reminder that our faith is a matter of life and death. Jesus constantly threatens the powers that be; following him puts us at odds with the same sort of folk who killed him.

But Stephen's life and martyrdom shine like a star in the night, like the Bethlehem star, guiding the wise past the fear of death and all the way to the place where Jesus is. "I see heavens opened and the Son of Man standing at the right hand of God" (Acts 7:56), Stephen says. His last words are, "Lord, do not hold this sin against them" (Acts 7:60), a prayer remarkable not only for its generosity but also because it sounds much like Jesus' last words.

Jesus' disciples are those who would die like him, with faith and forgiveness on their lips. They are those who would live like Jesus too: determined to speak as Jesus spoke. Christians are those who can boast that they have never said or done anything original.

On December 28 we celebrate the Feast of the Holy Innocents, those children who gave their lives for Jesus so that he could give his life for others. Matthew relates the terrible tale in three verses (2:16-18), as if to indicate that the evangelist himself barely had the stomach to tell it at all, how Herod in a rage has all the children in and around Bethlehem murdered. The magi, so foolish for all their wisdom, had visited the unstable king and told him they had seen a star, the herald of a new ruler for Israel. The king, fearful for all his power, sends his armies against the village's two-and-under toddlers. Their campaign succeeds with grim efficiency, but Herod's plan fails. Jesus, the newborn king, escapes. Many other children do not. These Holy Innocents cry out year by year that the message of Christmas goes far beyond a sentimental pageant for bathrobed shepherds in hand-towel headdresses to a dread drama with dirges as well as accompanying carols.

"The Word became flesh and lived among us" (John 1:14). If for Mary and Stephen and the Innocents that meant pain and blood and tears, for the powers and rulers of this world it means death in favor of God's new life.

Jesus first dwelt among us in the unlit darkness, the numbing cold of a Bethlehem night, there among smelly animals and all the smelly things stabled animals do. It was not a pristine moment, though the holiday greeting cards would like us to think otherwise. Few pristine moments will follow. At the beginning and at the end there is the tearing of skin, the pouring of blood, and screams of pain. The Word taking on Mary's flesh is a dangerous and untidy business. Following Jesus proves just as dangerous, just as untidy.

That some can welcome the Holy Family or the Holy One only sentimentally while others cannot welcome them at all comes as no surprise. Jesus' arrival makes a difference, creates a divide, breaks things in two: history, religions, hearts. There is joy but also sadness. There is life but also death. There is mercy but there is at the same time judgment, each attending the other. There is separation, as at Creation, and there is reconciliation for the making and remaking of the world. There is blood and pain and sometimes the rending of flesh—all for the healing and restoration of the nations.

The nations will be healed, the world restored. The zeal of the Lord of hosts will do this,

For a child has been born for us,
    a son given to us;
authority rests upon his shoulders;
    and he is named
Wonderful Counselor, Mighty God,
    Everlasting Father, Prince of Peace.
His authority shall grow continually,
    and there shall be endless peace. . . .
    from this time onward and forevermore (Isa. 9:6-7).

God does not retreat from our calamity. God does not abandon us to our self-destruction or leave us as food for the darkness. God comes and will come again. For amazingly, incredulously, God so loved the world.

Affirmation: Jesus' birth proves that God loves the broken world.

Confession: We doubt/ignore/reject God's love for the world.

Discipleship Task: To celebrate God's love for the world by making space in our lives to receive Jesus in all the ways he comes to us.

Advent

Christmas

Epiphany [Middle English *epiphanie,* from Anglo-French, from Late Latin *epiphania,* from Late Greek, plural, probably alteration of Greek *epiphaneia* appearance, manifestation, from *epiphainein* to manifest, from *epi-* + *phainein* to show] **1:** capitalized: January 6 observed as a church festival in commemoration of the coming of the Magi as the first manifestation of Christ to the Gentiles or in the Eastern Church in commemoration of the baptism of Christ **2:** an appearance or manifestation especially of a divine being **3a** (1): a usually sudden manifestation or perception of the essential nature or meaning of something

Lent

Holy Week

Easter

Pentecost

Trinity

Ordinary Time

Reign of Christ

3

From an Exclusive to an Inclusive Faith

EPIPHANY

Jesus loves the little children, all the children of the world:
Red and yellow, black and white, they are precious in his sight.
Jesus loves the little children of the world.

—ANONYMOUS

All parents know that sooner or later the time will come when their children will ask, "Where did I come from?" Some parents I have known, hoping to treat their little ones as adults, answer the questions biologically. They may say, "You came from your mother's belly" or "womb" and so proceed to give their children the cellular facts as best they can.

Other parents answer the question as they themselves might have been answered, more mythologically. "The stork brought you" or some such. Each answer works because it postpones further discussion to a later season, and many times that is what parents want. But in many other ways, neither answer works and does not tell inquiring children what they want to know. At least that is how a friend assessed the situation as she described the moment when her little girl asked, "Mommy, where was I before I was born?" My friend, in a moment of high inspiration, answered spiritually. Tears spilled as she said, "In the heart of God, honey. Before we knew you, you were in the heart of God. And we are so glad God gave you to us." Several months later she said they talked biology, but those facts were less important to her child than the truth, which is that she was a gift of God's heart, a sign of God's love.

My friend Ron says that the best conversations occur when the child is adopted, for then parents can answer theologically. When his son Chris asked the perennial question, Ron replied, "We chose you, Chris. We had always wanted a son, and God made it possible for us to have you. You were a gift." Perhaps all parents feel that way.

Other questions followed: "Who is my real mother? Did she not want me? What's wrong with me that she gave me away?" And yet, Ron said, as hard as those questions were, Chris seemed more or less content with the sharp edges of his story because he believed Ron when he said, "We chose you. We adopted you. We wanted you to be a part of our family."

∞

Epiphany offers the wondering world comparable loving testimony, tells us of God's plan from the beginning of the world to its end: to choose all of us, to unite all fractured humanity into one family, one people. Sadly, despite angelic announcements and prophetic pronouncements—indications now and then of God's ultimate will and purposes—many of God's children possess ears too deaf to hear all that God and the prophets have spoken. The fullness of God's gracious intent has often been muted, and even now among some it lies buried beneath landslides of tribalism, pride, and misunderstanding.

These are the words God first spoke to Abram: "I will make of you a great nation, and I will bless you, and make your name great, so that you will be a blessing. . . . and in you all the families of the earth shall be blessed" (Gen. 12:2-3). Across time and place, many of God's people remembered and trumpeted that first cluster of God's promises while minimizing—if not ignoring, qualifying, roping off with many requirements—the second.

For some generations of Abraham's heirs (and perhaps for some in *every* generation), to be "chosen" suggested special privilege and advantage, which is understandable. They had been entrusted with the land, the Law, and the Temple. God had called *them*, not others, and had made them a distinct people, set apart for the task of knowing and doing God's will. If they had been given a unique identity and work, no wonder many came to believe that they also had an exclusive and excluding relationship to God and God's will. God's requirements for them became their prerequisites for everyone else, and no outsider might imagine they could have audience with *their* God—or even come near the Temple—without a painful conversion to Judaism. And woe be to the born-Jew who intermarried or otherwise mingled with outsiders.

Not everyone held this understanding. Many of the prophets reminded the Israelites that God's grace was for all people; they were but the channels of that grace. Humility was to be their posture and service their means of bringing God's blessing into the world.

∽

All people were invited to the mountain to worship, a sign of God's borderless and everlasting peace. (Read Isaiah 25:6-9.) But even then, like now, not everyone wanted to hear that inclusive word. Some imagined God as their own possession, the blessing their particular right, and prosperity their inevitable destiny.

So it does not surprise us that even such a prophet as Jonah, called to preach in Nineveh in the east, sets sail for the west. God's insistent mercy proves stronger than Jonah's dissent. If in the darkness of the fish's belly Jonah does not see the light, when the fish coughs him up on the shore and God tells him once again to go preach in Nineveh, he does. Unenthusiastically, begrudging both the city's repentance and God's pardon. But Jonah proves to be a prophet of God's will in spite of himself; God loves not only repentant Ninevites but even defiant Israelites. God's mercy is God's to give, and over and over it is given to God's children.

What God shows Jonah, others have already seen. Isaiah called out that God would soon provide a "light to the nations" (42:6) so that salvation might reach the ends of the earth. The prophet foresaw a time when God's servant would call to nations he did not know, that untold nations would in turn run to him.

From the heart of God through the mouths of the prophets, the Word comes to our ears. From the foundations of the world to the skies over the Judean countryside, the Light comes to our eyes. From the manger in Bethlehem to all who see and follow the star—there is light, unveiling, enlightening. We discover divine treasure long hidden in the fields of time, good news for all people, to the Gentiles as well as the Jews, to the Jews no less than the Gentiles.

Epiphany, both the day (January 6) and the weeks-long season (until Ash Wednesday and the beginning of Lent), has been celebrated since the fourth century. It reminds us that God ultimately desires to bring all of God's children into the sphere of mercy and blessing—to unite all things in Christ, things in heaven and things on earth. God's radical hospitality obliterates every exclusion.

While the full scope of God's plan, along with the identity of the One who will accomplish it, has been largely hidden until now, Epiphany proclaims and celebrates God's gift to all people. No surprise then that the first and primary narrative for Epiphany is Matthew's story of the magi. On January 6 we celebrate their arrival at the home of Mary and Joseph. As God comes to the world in Jesus, the world comes to Jesus in the magi. Gentiles bring gifts to the Jew; Jews bring the gift of Christ to the Gentiles.

Visitors from the East come when Jesus is still in diapers, wise men who have foolishly announced to the reigning king that a baby has been born to usurp his throne. Tradition tells us that there were three wise men. Later tradition even assigns them names: Caspar, Melchior, and Balthazar. They show up as almost an afterthought, set dressing, the final act of the children's annual Christmas pageant. Because the play is already running long and the toddler-angels are getting fidgety and reaching for the chrismons, we rush the wise men to the manger's side, a regal denouement to the drama. The last to arrive, they are first to leave again. And in most churches' Nativity scene, the wise men stand next to the shepherds and gaze down on the newborn baby Jesus.

But the magi most likely arrived much later, as much as two years after Jesus' birth, given Herod's infanticidal decree. Their coming, their worship, sounds the first dramatic notes in a new movement of Jesus' life and God's purposes. These Gentile magi are a long way from where they might ever have imagined themselves to be, on a strange mission to bring gifts to a young stranger, a Hebrew male child, a great King. The gold, frankincense, and myrrh signal both their fealty and their faith in a reality beyond any conventional, political, or palatial wisdom.

The magi follow the star, a bright ball of grace in the West—a hole punched in the night. But not everyone does, and even those who notice do not recognize its significance. Its appearance is cryptic, an astrometric rune hidden in plain sight from the oblivious or inattentive. They travel by sheer faith—hard work with a dash of lunacy thrown in. Like Israel in the wilderness generations before, the magi pilgrims travel in search of a promise. Their worship signals the dawn of a new age that foreshadows the day when no shadows will exist, when no veils cover the eyes or ears of God's children, when all people will come to the mountain of God to feast and rejoice and sing praise.

The wise men come seeking Jesus. He comes to his own—his own world, his own people—and though many despise and reject him, many see him full of grace and truth. His natal star, like a flashlight in the hand of God, leads the magi up the dark and rocky path till it comes to where the child lay and glitters their believing eyes. The wise still come as testimony that he embodies the only hope for the dark, sad world.

The foolish wise men follow a star and, like the frightened shepherds who saw the glory of the Lord shining all around them, make their way to the One who will bring light in the darkness, peace in the chaos, oasis in the wilderness, and company along the way. We too, though just as foolish and frightened, may find that he is "the hope of all who seek him, the help of all who find."

The Gentile sages fulfill Isaiah's prophecy in their coming and thereby raise the curtain on a new season in the Christian year—Epiphany. The name, a transliteration of a Greek word that means "unveiling," tells the story of how the one born King of the Jews is also Savior of the world. God so loved *the world* that God sent Jesus.

The church exists to reiterate that message, full as it is of grace and comfort and also of prophetic warning and challenge, to the powers and principalities of this world. The magi, kings of the earth, came to Jesus. This is the first story of Epiphany. The stories that follow tell of Jesus' going into the world proclaiming the kingdom of God, good news for all who will welcome it, of God's coming reign over all the earth.

∞

Jesus told parables. We do not read far in the New Testament before Jesus' stories, riddles, and vignettes confront us—a man has two sons; a sower goes out to sow; a woman misplaces a coin; a shepherd loses a sheep. "With many such parables [Jesus] spoke the word," the Gospel of Mark tells us. It goes on to say that Jesus "did not speak to them except in parables, but he explained everything in private to his disciples" (4:33-34). Because Jesus' meaning is not always obvious, the parables require explanation.

"'Which one of you, having a hundred sheep and losing one of them, does not leave the ninety-nine in the wilderness and go after the one that is lost until he finds it?" (Luke 15:4). Well, *no* shepherd does that, frankly. Most shepherds would consider a 1 percent loss acceptable and, especially in savage environs, would work to protect the others. But not this shepherd. He leaves his flock alone in the wild and goes after one sheep. *One!* The Good Shepherd will not willingly suffer the loss of any of those entrusted to him, though it endangers both his followers and himself to seek and save the lost sheep.

The woman who misplaces the coin finds it and then spends more on the party than she lost to begin with. The foolish sower slings seed everywhere and thereby proves God's wisdom. The father, whose younger son has wished him dead, welcomes him back with festival and song, much to the chagrin of his older son who has remained faithful all along.

Jesus spins his tales; some have the ears to hear and eyes to see, but some do not. "As it was in the beginning, is now, and ever shall be." Even those who want to understand don't. The kingdom of God is like new wine, like treasure buried in a field. It is like a mustard seed or yeast in three measures of flour. It is like birth, like death, like the wind. Jesus tells parables, and a scholar I used to know would say that they are like a good joke—if you get it, you really get it; it opens your eyes. If you don't get it, you feel blinder, deafer, dumber than you already know yourself to be.

Parables tell the truth, but they tell it "slant," as Emily Dickinson wrote in her poem "Tell all the truth but tell it slant."[1] The kingdom of God is like a bush with lots of different birds singing lots of different songs. It is like a fig tree. It is like a vineyard. The parables "dazzle us gradually" as Dickinson advises so that bolts of lightning do not rend our darkness. No, the surprise of truth comes more like fingers of dawn at the far edge of our incomprehension as a promise of incremental understanding. The light gradually enables us, bit by bit, to see. A parable resembles the sunrise for those who are awake and looking.

Jesus tells parables. He also *is* a parable in his life and ministry, in the things he does and the things that happen around him. For those with eyes to see, it all seems a kind of slant truth-telling. God's grace remains unbound by time, Jesus says, and proves as much when he heals on the sabbath. God does not limit divine regard to some. Jesus *heals* on the sabbath, *teaches* women the Law. He talks to a *Samaritan* woman in public and makes a Samaritan man the hero of one of his most recounted stories. Jesus breaks the conventional taboos for the sake of life and healing and the kingdom.

The religious leaders grow increasingly furious and determine to stop him, to put him to death if need be. Jesus does his work in public— "Stretch out your withered hand for all to see" (Mark 3:5, AP) he tells the man in the synagogue. But Jesus' opponents do their work in secret, keep their withered hearts hidden and safe from his healing touch.

Jesus touches a leper who desires healing. Earlier that day Jesus healed Simon's mother-in-law, and word spread so quickly that at sundown—the start of a new day—the whole town brings their sick in hopes Jesus will heal them too. And he does. But the next morning, a long time before daylight, Jesus gets up and goes to a lonely place to pray. As he seeks the Father, the disciples hunt for the Son. After finding him, they say, "We have to go back and do that again." Jesus said, "We have to go on ahead, so that I can preach in the next towns, for *that* is what I came to do" (Mark 1:38, AP).

Jesus is casting out demons and proclaiming the message when the leper comes to him and states, "If you choose, you can make me clean" (Mark 1:40). Our Bibles say that Jesus is moved with pity when he sees the man. He chooses on the basis of compassion to heal him. As noted in study Bible footnotes for Mark 1:41, many Greek manuscripts state that Jesus' emotional reaction to the leper's request is anger. The leper interrupts Jesus' stated mission, but Jesus chooses to heal him anyway. To heal this unfortunate man, Jesus sacrifices his own desire.

The story exemplifies the way Jesus alters his itinerary, takes another action, spends himself in a new way for the sake of the one who asks. He casts his lot with outsiders, calling many of his disciples from the fringe. Jesus comes to his own, over and over again, choosing them, taking his righteous place even among the unrighteous.

∞

Jesus comes to the Jordan River to receive baptism from his cousin, John. The Baptizer has set up prophetic shop far from what he considers the corrupt precincts of Jerusalem and its temple, its maculate priests and practices. John takes his place down by the riverside and Jesus comes there too, standing shoulder-to-shoulder with the riffraff and sinners, the vipers and snakes John routinely excoriated. All of these desire water baptism as a sign of repentance, but what they really need, John says, is fire baptism and real repentance, gifts neither he nor the river can give. They need a bathing deeper than Jordan's reach, a subcutaneous watering to let these barren and withered "trees" bring forth worthy fruit. And when Jesus wades into the Jordan for baptism, John tries to prevent him, saying, "I need to be baptized by you, and do you come to me?" (Matt. 3:13).

Yes. John, like the rest of them, needs the gift that only Jesus can give. Jesus shows himself Messiah and Savior, Son of Man and Son of God as he who needs neither baptism nor repentance comes to those who need both. He came to the Jordan that day, and he comes today to fonts and baptisteries and riversides because he is not afraid to be known by the company he keeps and because he keeps company with God. Jesus comes for baptism, and John would prevent him; but Jesus says, "Let it be so now; for it is proper for us in this way to fulfill all righteousness" (Matt. 3:15).

Righteousness has all of them taking their proper places: John in the water, the crowds by the riverside, and Jesus with the crowds—not above them, lording himself over the citizens of his kingdom but beside them, among them, shoulder-to-shoulder and cross-to-cross. Though the people do not realize who is in their midst, still he loves them and serves them. He knows they will soon reject him, but still he comes to the Jordan, taking his righteous place for and with the unrighteous. Emmanuel, doing God's will and fulfilling his own purpose by taking his dusty place, his damp with water or blood place, lowered there by another's hands into the river and the tomb.

As Jesus comes up out of the water, there is a dove, but not everyone sees it. There is a voice, but not everyone hears it or understands. Jesus sees and comprehends. He understands full well who he is but not yet all of what that might mean. And so, with his baptism still dripping off his chin, he strides into the wilderness—thrown into the wilderness, the Greek text says—there to be tempted by Satan. The tempter understands well enough who Jesus is and so tries to subvert his mission.

"Command these stones to be made bread. Satisfy your own shrinking belly and the hunger of your people. That's what good kings do, after all; they feed the people" (Matt. 4:3, AP).

"Cast yourself down—amaze the masses and prove who you are by demonstrations of self-serving, self-protecting power. That's what the people want, after all—bread and circuses" (Matt. 4:6, AP).

"Worship me—God can have the world. Take this shortcut to where you are headed anyway. If you are—since you are—the Son of God, prove it" (Matt. 4:9, AP).

Jesus refuses each time, but the temptations are real, the logic credible. All Jesus' tempters, even his own disciples then and now, ask him the same thing in one form or another: "If you are . . . since you are . . . prove it. Let me see your power by what you give me." But saying no to the tempter and his ways helps Jesus—and us—say yes to God and God's ways.

∞

One day a large crowd follows Jesus. In late afternoon the tired disciples suggest that Jesus dismiss the people so they can go to the neighboring villages and buy food. They want to keep Jesus for themselves. He is their Lord; they are his servants. Their concern has boundaries, limits—it doesn't include everyone. But Jesus will have none of it. When Jesus tells them, "You give them something to eat" (Matt. 14:16), he relays the word that the crowds are part of the family and have a place at the table. Even if the disciples understand that part of it, they don't see how all the people can be fed. "There is a boy here who has five barley loaves and two fish" (John 6:9), Andrew notes. "But what are they among so many people?" The disciples see only scarcity: what they don't have, what they can't do.

Jesus, the gracious host, has the people sit down. He blesses the food—and there is plenty. More than enough for everyone. So much that they gather the leftovers in baskets. Some scholars read this text and say those very loaves and fish were miraculously multiplied. But other scholars suggest that when people witness the boy's offering and Jesus' blessing of his food, they begin sharing their bag lunches too, suddenly neither too afraid nor too selfish to do so.

If in the first interpretation the miracle is unique and unrepeatable, bespeaking Jesus' compassion and power; in the second the miracle is repeatable and fashioned from Jesus' power to change not just loaves but our hearts as well. When we follow the example of faith exhibited in the boy's generosity and give our best to Jesus and each other, we find we have more than enough to spare. When we let go of our fear, when we see the stranger as neighbor, the outsider as insider—all of that hard work, to be sure—we find that our desire to do as Jesus does blesses others. It fills empty stomachs and softens hard hearts. It softens our hearts when we leave exclusion behind.

∞

Sometime after John's arrest, Jesus marches into Galilee to proclaim the gospel of the kingdom of God: "The time is fulfilled, and the kingdom of God has come near; repent, and believe in the good news" (Mark 1:14). Everyone can repent. Everyone *has* to repent. Neither blessing nor warning is exclusive.

Tax collectors hear the message and know that profit is not wage enough to exchange for a life. Fishermen hear and suddenly know that life can no longer consist of nets, baits, and boats and what they catch from beneath the surface of the sea. Not after Jesus has hooked them deep in their hearts.

Simon and Andrew wade in the shallows and cast their nets. It is a parable, this description of the two sets. James and John have a boat, or at least their father, Zebedee, does, and they have helpers too, hired hands. They work the deeper waters. Are the four fishermen competitors? rivals? enemies? The text does not tell us. The text does tell us that Jesus passes by the Sea of Galilee and sees the four of them, two by two. He calls. They follow, and the hardest learning commences.

The early morning mist of Galilee's sea settles over clarity and, except for the weather and the haul, predictability. Everyone acknowledges the pecking order. Simon and Andrew have their favorite spot, while James and John know where to dock. They fathom the language and the layout, the customs and the customers, the routine and its reasons. Leaving the mist to follow Jesus means entering a veritable fog, and for three years they do not know what to think or do, what to say or to whom. They have to learn a new way of talking, of thinking, of relating to each other and everyone else.

Jesus keeps confusing them: "The one who has it all has nothing; the one who has nothing on account of me is rich beyond accounting. Those who are not for us are against us; those who are not against us are for us. You have learned to do what Moses said; I am telling you to do more and better" (AP).

Jesus invites others to join the group—a Roman collaborator *and* a political revolutionary set on the occupation's overthrow. Uncertainty and confusion reigns; those invited can discern no pecking order since Jesus loves them all. He seems to expect each of them to love all the others, just as he does, and so they try to learn.

Jesus and his first disciples, the four fishermen, begin traveling together. One day the five of them go to Capernaum. Jesus teaches in the synagogue and then goes to the home of Simon and Andrew where Jesus heals Simon's mother-in-law. Mark tells us that Jesus, along with Simon and Andrew, "entered the house . . . with James and John" (1:29), and we might wonder why the Gospel makes a point of it. After all, Jesus and these two have been together for several verses now, and no reader would picture it otherwise. Or does Mark want us to take note? Following Jesus means we travel with people we might never have imagined—competitors and rivals and even enemies now become friends.

Following Jesus entails entering homes that we might have avoided before—my home is your home and your home is mine.

Following Jesus means we reject rejection, drop old distinctions, and abandon prejudice.

We will be known by a new company and a borderless geography and a fresh way of looking at people and things. We have all things in common—friends, resources, homes—because we have Jesus in common.

Nothing more than him. And by grace nothing less.

But this reorientation of relationships and values is hard. Jesus called tax collectors and Zealots, the educated and the unschooled. He dined with the religious authorities and brought with him others who had trouble with authority. He felt equally at home in the presence of Pharisees and prostitutes.

The kingdom of God, he says, is like a net holding all sorts of fish. He could have said the kingdom of God is like the ark where predators and prey occupy the same cage—but the Flood canceled all bets, changed things, reconfigured all relationships. The kingdom of God overflows Judaism's banks and overturns the customary ways of relating. Likely friends turn out to be enemies. Old enemies are new friends.

∞

One day Jesus, Peter, James, and John climb up a mountainside. Jesus is transfigured before them. What that means exactly, only the four of them know for sure, but one way or the other, something remarkable happens. Jesus' clothes and flesh and presence glow so that he no longer looks human. Suddenly Moses and Elijah stand talking with him about Jesus' departure when he will climb another mountain, alone this time except for the soldiers and the others bearing crosses. He will be transfigured again—again, he will not look human—his flesh torn and his blood all but bled out, ruined beyond recognition.

Moses and Jesus and Elijah are talking about all of that when Peter says, "Master, it is good for us to be here" (Luke 9:33), by which maybe he means it is better to be *here* than to be *there*, if he has any sense of where *there* was or why they were headed that way. The text states that he did not know what he was saying when he suggested, "Let us make three dwellings, one for you, one for Moses, and one for Elijah" (Luke 9:33).

It's as if Peter is saying, "We like it here. We like how this feels. This is what being a disciple is all about. Forget the world below. This little enclave is sufficient unto itself."

Jesus doesn't fuss, but neither can he stay; they will have to follow him if they want to be with him. So they leave and go down the mountain, the glow having dissipated.

When the group reaches the bottom, they discover that in Jesus' absence the remaining disciples have been unable to help the epileptic son of a distraught father. An argument has erupted, and Jesus seems annoyed, as if he too would rather be back on the mountain than there dealing with the situation. The man says to Jesus, "I asked your disciples to cast [the spirit] out, but they could not do so. . . . If you are able to do anything, have pity on us and help us" (Mark 9:18, 22). It is as if the man has seen so much of the incompetence of Jesus' followers that he doubts Jesus' abilities.

"'If you are able!'" Jesus snorts. As if to say to the man, Do you have any idea to whom you are talking? "'All things can be done for the one who believes'" (Mark 9:23). All things are possible for Jesus, for he is the one, the only one, who *does* believe. The man, to his credit, admits what all of us need to confess—that all things are not possible because we do not all believe or do not believe it all: "I believe; help my unbelief!" (Mark 9:24).

Jesus works the miracle. His disciples prove themselves unable to do what Jesus has given them the authority to do: heal.

Jesus then walks on ahead while the disciples argue among themselves. When he asks them what they are arguing about, they get very quiet, embarrassed, for they were arguing as to who was the greatest.

Sometime after that, John tells Jesus, "Teacher, we saw someone casting out demons in your name, and we tried to stop him, because he was not following us" (Mark 9:38). The irony cannot be more overwhelming: The disciples cannot do or prevent others from doing, but they still argue about who among them is the greatest. We hear the echo of Jesus' lament, "You faithless generation, how much longer must I be among you? How much longer must I put up with you?" (Mark 9:19).

Only to the end, as it turns out. "Having loved his own who were in the world, he loved them to the end" (John 13:1). An amazing grace. A merciful hospitality.

∞

In many places I visit, I see the poem "Footprints in the Sand" by Mary Stevenson Zangare. The climax and comfort come at the end when Jesus says, "The times when you have seen only one set of footprints in the sand, is when I carried you."

Yes, yes. I understand and believe. When we are in the wilderness, when we are down and low, when we are anguished and sorrowful and defeated, Jesus does indeed carry us. That is the consolation of our faith.

But I have been thinking that many of us desire only consolation from our faith. We want comfort, assurance, healing, and health. We want God to bless us "real good," to expand our territory, to rapture us away from here when the going gets tough. We want to be carried, one way or the other, one place to the other. So we like the image of just one set of footprints in the sand. We like Jesus being our "personal" Savior.

But Jesus comes to the Sea of Galilee, preaching the gospel of God. He calls—and four answer. Four follow Jesus, adding their footprints to his on the sand. If we want to envision what it means to follow Jesus, it is this: footprints in the sand, many sets of footprints. We see not one set, not him carrying us but many sets of footprints—seeking him, finding him, following him. The magi, the man with the withered hand, the fishermen, all of their feet moving toward Jesus, his grace the gravity that pulls them close and keeps them there.

For a while anyway.

Affirmation: Jesus is not only King of the Jews but Savior of *the world.*

Confession: We want Jesus to be ours alone (self, church, nation).

Discipleship Task: To see how Jesus loves *the world* and to follow him by moving from an exclusive to an inclusive faith.

Advent

Christmas

Epiphany

Lent [Middle English *lente* springtime, Lent, from Old English *lencten*; akin to Old High German *lenzin* spring]: the 40 weekdays from Ash Wednesday to Easter observed by the Roman Catholic, Eastern, and some Protestant churches as a period of penitence and fasting

Holy Week

Easter

Pentecost

Trinity

Ordinary Time

Reign of Christ

4

From Entitlement to Selflessness

LENT

Mortification is the intentional denial of legitimate pleasures
in the spirit of Christian poverty that one might become more
human. In my tradition Lent has long been considered a time
for mortification, although one would not use such a "medieval"
word. We gave up eating desserts, going to movies, or telling dirty
jokes, all of which in the face of world problems seemed rather
trivial. Once rendered silly, we dismissed the idea of "giving up"
and talked of "taking on." What we failed to understand was
that a life incapable of significant sacrifice is also incapable of
courageous action.

—Urban T. Holmes III

The day of Jesus' circumcision, Simeon can see it all coming—the
blood and the tears, the war and the peace, the wounds and the
healing—and all of it so clearly he knows he can die happy.

"Master," Simeon prays as he holds the baby Jesus toward heaven, "now you are dismissing your servant in peace, according to your word" (Luke 2:29). Others have dismissed him as well, and who can blame them? Prophets serve without honor in their own precincts, especially if those precincts belong to the Temple.

I picture Simeon as an old man for some reason, with bits of food in his beard, tattered robes, and wild eyes. Does he come to the Temple every day or just *that* day? He awaits a sign, believing he will see the Lord's Christ before he tastes death.

I also imagine that most of the faithful who frequent the Temple ignore Simeon as best they can, discounting both his presence and his prescience, his predictions and his prayers.

Eight days after Jesus' birth, as Luke tells us, Mary and Joseph bring their infant son to Jerusalem for circumcision in accordance with the Law. That same day Simeon comes to the Temple and sees them, the Holy Family. Mary and Joseph's faithfulness to the customs handed down since the time of Abraham bring Jesus to the city and to this moment in the Temple. Simeon's trust in the Holy Spirit's words, his hope for Israel and the world, prompt him to greet the Holy Family as they arrive.

Simeon takes the child from Mary's arms and, one imagines, begins to dance and sing a glad, new song to God: "My eyes have seen your salvation, which you have prepared in the presence of all peoples, a light for revelation to the Gentiles and for glory to your people Israel" (Luke 2:30-32).

Does anyone else notice the old man, listen to his song, take note of his dance, and wonder what it all might mean? Mary and Joseph must shiver as Simeon sings and capers about. *They* know who their Son is but are unaware that anyone beyond Bethlehem's shepherds do. They *know* he is set apart for God's work, but they are not yet certain what that work will entail. But Simeon sees it all: the light and the glory . . . and also the darkness and shame.

Simeon's face suddenly loses its smile, his feet their rhythm. Tears remain in his eyes and on his cheeks as he holds Jesus close to his chest and warns, "This child is destined for the falling and the rising of many in Israel, and to be a sign that will be opposed" (Luke 2:34). Simeon can already envision the wars of words, the resentments and rejections, the end. He realizes that this ritual wounding in the Temple is but the first

Jesus will suffer at the hands of the religious leaders, these drops but the first blood he will spill in obedience to God's command.

"And a sword will pierce your own soul too" (Luke 2:35), Simeon now tells Mary, who must have shivered again. Her baby's life is too fresh for her to consider his death. Nor can she yet conceive that her child, flesh of her flesh, is appointed to an ancient and dangerous work. Who can imagine this baby's end? Certainly not his mother.

Simeon will die in peace, but the child will not. I suspect Simeon understands that as well. Jesus' death will give way to life, and Simeon can die in peace. Any time now.

∞

Lent begins on Ash Wednesday, a little over six and one-half weeks before Easter. It is a season apart, a tithe of the year as some have called it, a time to give ourselves, join ourselves more closely to Jesus. We remember that the one born King of the Jews and Savior of the world will suffer to do God's will in the world and that those who follow him must suffer with him and die with him if it comes to that.

"If the world hates you, be aware that it hated me before it hated you" (John 15:18), Jesus warns his followers. "If any want to become my followers, let them deny themselves and take up their cross daily and follow me" (Luke 9:23). We take up the cross daily, but for this period we call Lent we take it up even more, or try to.

At the altar my parishioners kneel, and on each forehead I smudge dark gray ash—what is left of the fronds we used last Palm Sunday, burned for this very purpose. I say to each in turn, "From dust you came, to dust you shall return. Repent and believe the gospel." My ashen touch reminds them, first, that we and the whole world are dust, that everything we consider permanent will be ash at the last. And, second, we must live our lives accordingly. Our very act of kneeling to receive the ashes serves as a confession that most days we live otherwise.

"Do not store up for yourselves treasures on earth" (Matt. 6:19), Jesus tells us, but we often do.

"Whoever has two coats must share with anyone who has none" (Luke 3:11), says John the Baptizer, but we most often do not.

"Blessed are you who are poor. . . . Woe to you who are rich" (Luke 6:20, 24), Jesus notes, but our brokers have convinced us otherwise.

We imagine ourselves as needy sometimes, but Lent demands that we tell the truth: Most of us have more than we need and are loathe to share the least of what we have.

A rich man suffers a crisis of plenty. (See Luke 12:16-21.) His fields produce a record crop, and he has nowhere to store the abundance. Perplexed as to what to do, he builds new barns and thanks God that while many struggle to make ends meet, he has enough to live well and die comfortably. "I wish everyone had as much as I," he might have said and sincerely considered himself blessed.

Jesus calls him a fool, and I nod condescending assent. How easy to see this man's silliness and presumption: We cannot serve God and money; God's blessings are to be shared. "Do not judge," Jesus said, "but consider your own sin before you see the sin of another" (Matt. 7:1, AP). We are all rich fools, truth be told, though sometimes we pretend we are otherwise. Lent's imperative, however, is that we confess our own silliness and presumption, identify and repent of the crookedness in us. Lent demands we acknowledge both that we need straightening and that we cannot straighten ourselves.

We cannot bring down the mountains of pride and entitlement that ward our hearts, cannot fill the deep moats of fear and greed that both protect our *stuff* and separate us from our needy neighbors. So we come to the altar to pray. To remember who we are and are not, who we are called to be and whom we are called to serve. We set ourselves apart during this time to begin a season of hard, sacrificial work in hopes that by grace we can move or be moved from pride to humility, from presumption to repentance, from judgment to confession. Lent calls us to leave our self-serving and our sense of entitlement behind us and to follow Jesus by setting our face toward selflessness and sacrifice. "Though [Jesus] was in the form of God," Paul writes, "[he] did not regard equality with God as something to be exploited, but emptied himself, . . . and became obedient to the point of death" (Phil. 2:6-8). We try to do likewise. We pray that God's goodness will so fill us that we want for nothing else, especially the doomed treasures of the world. We make a small hole in our lives, open a crack in our days, give up something for the sake of him who gave up everything so that a bit of light might seep in, that holiness be born in us.

What can we give to the God who has all? Only what we take from ourselves. Our small sacrifice helps us develop a patterned obedience, a willful sacrifice. When we take something away from our lives and give it to God, we create space. We rely, in one more way, on God's sufficiency.

∞

Thursday night in the Steagald house was always vocabulary night. For years, one or the other of the kids had a vocabulary test on Friday morning, and early on we got into a pattern of preparation. We would take blank index cards, and on one side of each she would write a word in big, block letters. On the other side she would write the definition of the word. She would then begin the work, showing first the word or its definition, then having the children call back to her the other.

Jesus adopts a similar strategy with his disciples in view of the coming test. In Caesarea Philippi, a town far north of Jerusalem, Jesus begins coaching, teaching, schooling his friends on what awaits them all—but especially awaits him. He gives them definitions, calls out words, tries to teach them what they need to know.

The city of Caesarea sits on a bustling crossroads—trade routes from here to there intersecting. Many kinds of people from sundry places and varying worship styles make Caesarea a different kind of place, and the local chamber of commerce attempts to make everybody feel right at home. No surprise then to find numerous churches, temples, and shrines, and plenty of attendant pluralism and tolerance.

In the midst of this syncretism, Jesus asks the disciples this question: "Who do people say that I am?" (Mark 8:27). The disciples offer several suggestions, trying to guess what everyone else's index card has on the back. Then Jesus asks yet another question: "But who do you say that I am?" (Mark 8:29).

"You are the Messiah" (Mark 8:29), Simon Peter replies.

Simon Peter is 100 percent correct. "Blessed are you, Simon son of Jonah! For flesh and blood has not revealed this to you, but my Father in heaven" (Matt. 16:17). Simon gets a gold star and a smiley face. And now that he knows the words, Jesus as much as says, "Let's turn the card over and learn the definition."

Jesus begins to teach his disciples the definition of Messiah, referring to himself as the Son of Man. "The Son of Man must undergo great suffering, and be rejected by the elders, the chief priests, and the scribes, and be killed, and after three days rise again." Jesus says this "quite openly" (Mark 8:31-32). But Peter does not like this lesson—doesn't like it for Jesus or for himself. He takes Jesus aside and rebukes him in words to this effect: "Quit talking like that. You are not going to Jerusalem, and you are not going to die."

Although Jesus willingly chooses to suffer at the hands of the elders, the priests, and others, he is unwilling to suffer such foolishness as this. He pushes right back, changing Peter's grade to a failing mark: "Get behind me, Satan! For you are setting your mind not on divine things but on human things" (Mark 8:33). Peter cannot "get" the definition on the back of the Son-of-Man card.

How like Peter we are. We too would love for Jesus' identity to offer protection and benefit to disciples—then and now—and it does, but not in the way Jesus' disciples often imagine. We are drawn to the blessings of following Jesus, not the cost. We covet the security, not the risk. We find ourselves tempted to imagine that our faithfulness and devotion provide tangible rewards. "Nothing too good for the servants of the Lord," we might say to ourselves, which is also to say, "Nothing too bad for the servants of the Lord." We do not want to believe that following Jesus can mean suffering and sacrifice.

∞

On Ash Wednesday, during my meditation and right before the imposition of ashes, I take from the pulpit a gift given me by a priest: a small black cross inlaid with twenty or thirty pieces of a shattered mirror. I place the cross on a little stand that people pass on their way to and from the imposition of ashes. When people look at the cross closely, they see themselves, but broken.

Indeed, all of us are broken. The cross on the stand, like the crosses in our sanctuaries, shows us that. We experience a disconnect between head and heart, between heart and life. My guilt is double because I know better—or should. Lent allows me, compels me, to confess how my theological precision grows dull and rusty, how the storehouse of my heavenly treasure is home to rats, how my convictions leak and muddy my prayers.

∞

Not everyone wants a suffering Messiah. Not everyone desires God's peculiar form of prosperity: The one who is poor is rich, the one who is a failure is a success, the one who is rejected is accepted, the one who would be first of all must be last of all and servant of all.

Mountains do not want to be brought low, and those who easily walk crooked roads are not eager for the bulldozers to appear. No surprise then that opposition and rejection, quarrels and contention, attend Jesus' mission almost from the start.

Among the most unsettling of Jesus' quarrels comes from his own disciples. Over and over again they either do not understand or they understand well enough but are reluctant, even resistant, to follow where he leads. They hear his words but do not allow them to sink deeper than that. Though time and time again Jesus tries to tell them that his suffering is inevitable, even necessary—and that their own sacrifices are part of a disciple's job description—they do not want to believe or follow in that way. They imagine that being intimate associates of the Messiah entitles them to certain perks, payoffs, benefits, and protections.

One day James and John ask Jesus, "Grant us to sit, one at your right and one at your left, in your glory" (Mark 10:37). Neither James nor John realize that Jesus' coronation will be his crucifixion; to be at his right or left means being crucified with him. "Those who find their life will lose it" (Matt. 10:39). Well, where is the fun in that?

∞

Sometime after his baptism and time of testing in the wilderness, Jesus returns to his hometown of Nazareth. He has been preaching for a while already and has received some acclaim and recognition. So not surprisingly when he goes to synagogue on the sabbath, he is given the scroll of Isaiah from which to read. He finds and reads the following passage:

The Spirit of the Lord is upon me,
because he has anointed me to bring good news to the poor.
He has sent me to proclaim release to the captives
and recovery of sight to the blind,
to let the oppressed go free,
to proclaim the year of the Lord's favor. (Luke 4:18-19)

Everyone in the synagogue likes this passage, but when Jesus begins preaching, matters turn ugly. His listeners think, *Do here what you did in Capernaum. After all, you are home now and that is where charity begins. Bless your kinfolk first; take care of those nearest to you.*

However, Jesus reminds his friends and kin that God healed a *Syrian* king's leprosy and did not heal the many Israelite lepers. There is no border on God's grace, he as much as says. He recalls that during a great famine God sent the prophet Elijah to feed a Gentile widow living in Sidon of Zarephath, while Israelite widows went hungry. God supports no special privilege or entitlement for one group over another—that seems the gist of his message for the day. No special protection for those who are called.

At the beginning of the sermon, all in the synagogue look at Jesus favorably and consider his words gracious. By the end, their rage at his preaching such a message forces them to attempt to throw him off a cliff.

But Jesus "passed through the midst of them" and goes on his way. Moses' parting the Red Sea seems no more miraculous, a professor of mine used to say. Soon though, the sea of Jesus' enemies will close round him again, and he will not escape.

Many of Jesus' sermons and stories, many of his miracles and the places he performed them, lay a parabolic ax to the root of long-assumed certainties. Jesus compares the religious leaders to wicked tenants, while hookers and tax collectors stand first in line at the kingdom's door. Though some have said yes to God's call and command, they have failed to fulfill their promise. Others have said no, yet obey in spite of themselves.

Jesus' perspective retains the hope that a new shoot of faithfulness, trellised by the Spirit more than the law, by mercy more than justice, will grow up among God's people. We do not have to guess, however, how the Pharisees and the Sadducees regarded Jesus' teaching. Or how they planned to deal with it.

"[They] went out and immediately conspired . . . how to destroy him" (3:6), Mark tells us. And if Jesus and the religious leaders can see it coming—as Simeon had long years before—Jesus' followers for the most part cannot begin to imagine what is about to transpire.

Affirmation: Jesus is a "sign that will be opposed" (Luke 2:34) as his ministry proves dangerous.

Confession: We want Jesus to ensure our success, wealth, and health.

Discipleship Task: To hear the call to self-denial and to follow Jesus by moving from entitlement to selflessness.

Advent

Christmas

Epiphany

Lent

Holy Week: the week before Easter during which
the last days of Christ's life are commemorated

Easter

Pentecost

Trinity

Ordinary Time

Reign of Christ

5

From Fear to Surrender

HOLY WEEK

How can we serve a Lord, the symbol of whose failure is above our altars, on top of our churches, on our stationery, and around our necks, and claim to be a stranger to failure?

—URBAN T. HOLMES III

The cross is such a hard, hard piece of the gospel that most of us cannot stay converted to it for long.

—BARBARA BROWN TAYLOR

Holy Week resembles the rest of Lent, only more intense. Every day brings a story of conflict. Every day a drama of redemption plays out. The fear that has accompanied the disciples along the way heightens. Everyone is afraid—the authorities, the disciples, and perhaps even Jesus.

Jesus "set his face to go to Jerusalem" (Luke 9:51), knowing full well what awaits him there. He moves past his fear to surrender—"not my will, but yours be done" (Luke 22:42)—and he expects that his disciples will move past their fear in order to follow.

Jesus has warned them: "Let these sayings sink down into your ears; the Son of man shall be delivered into [human hands]" (Luke 9:44, KJV). But the warning does not suffice. The disciples' fear remains. They do not ask Jesus what he means. They do not want to know.

Palm/Passion Sunday: The Triumphal Entry

Tell the daughter of Zion,

> Lo, your king comes to you;
> . . . humble and riding on a donkey,
>   on a colt, the foal of a donkey. (Zechariah 9:9)

Matthew reads Zechariah's prophecy literally. He tells us that the disciples bring both a donkey and a colt to Jesus and put their cloaks on them. Jesus rides astraddle both of them on his descent into Jerusalem. We can picture this attempt—different heights, different gaits. Jesus bounces along, trying hard to maintain his balance.

We also try to stay astride both Palm Sunday truths: Jesus is coming at last, but he is coming to die. Do we celebrate? Do we cry? Are we happy? Are we afraid?

Yes.

∞

Father Charles comes to the community Palm Sunday service in a flowing red cape that billows out behind him in the breeze. He is a very large man, and the cape is larger. He seems to fly or float through the crowd gathered in the middle of Main Street to hear and read the Palm Sunday scriptures.

Red: the color of festival, of fire and celebration—Jesus comes to Jerusalem! Behold your King! The other ministers and I appear underdressed, out of sync with Father Charles and this news. Soon, though, when the mood and the lessons shift from red to purple and black (as we read accounts of the trial, the suffering, the death of Jesus), Father Charles will be the one overdressed, out of sync, unless the red flowing down his back and pooling at his feet represents blood.

Father Charles in his red, me in my purple, Herb and Jerry in their black suits. Festivity and mourning, celebration and lamentation, all of it together this day. Jesus is King; an assassination plot is underway. It is hard to ride the mismatched realities brought to us this day. We feel unbalanced, unsettled, unsure as to what it all means.

We do not know, not all of it anyway; and like Jesus' disciples we often fear to ask what goes on here.

∞

Jesus begins to descend the Mount of Olives and the disciples begin "to praise God joyfully with a loud voice for all the deeds of power that they had seen" (Luke 19:37). They sing, they dance; they whoop it up big. The parade may be small, but the festivity drives some of the Pharisees to tell Jesus to get control of his disciples. "Order your disciples to stop" (Luke 19:39). They as much as say, "This display is unseemly." Jesus replies, "If these were silent, the stones would shout out" (Luke 19:40). And so they will, so they will.

Soon an earthquake will stir the city. Everyone, disciples and enemies alike, will lose their footing, lose their sight, be scared almost to death. Or to life.

As Jesus draws near Jerusalem, he cries over it. "If you, even you, had only recognized on this day the things that make for peace!" (Luke 19:41). Jesus weeps because only one thing can make for peace, and it means the ruin of him. Jesus weeps because his enemies stand ready to do that ruinous work, imagining that his solitary suffering will somehow save the nation.

The people seem to desire a king like David, a warrior who will bring peace through war, freedom through victory, the death of Israel's occupiers and enemies. Jesus offers peace through surrender, freedom through defeat, and life for all by his willingness to die.

Jesus on a donkey. He is on a protest march though even the disciples do not realize it at first. Jesus protests the grandiose and militaristic expectations of those who learn to translate *Messiah* in terms of stallions and swords and wars. The parade is a funeral procession too, though Jesus alone seems to understand this.

Jesus does not explain his actions; he does not justify or interpret them. He remains silent, keeps his own counsel, though the world is abuzz around him. Some are frenzied, others panicked. Some say he is the Son of David, the King of the Jews. Others say he is an imposter, a pretender, an insurrectionist. Some hail him, others rebuke him; some want to crown him, others want to kill him.

But Jesus says not a word.

He allows the crowds, his friends and enemies, to make of him what they will—a king, a criminal, a victim, or even a sacrifice. He still does.

Monday: The Confrontation in the Temple

John tells the story of Jesus' confrontation in the Temple early in his Gospel, right after the wedding in Cana. John sounds a tone, playing an overture whose themes will come later: Following Jesus involves both wine-drinking good times and blood-chilling confrontations. Followers will experience no joy greater than the joy of being with Jesus and no danger more ominous than being his disciple. Following him brings peace; following him brings conflict.

We can imagine the disciples' vacillating emotions. Elated, perhaps, about their teacher being the life of the party, able to make a fine pinot out of plain old well water. Terrified when Jesus makes a whip of cords and starts chasing the money changers out of the Temple. I can see the disciples huddle in the corner, out of harm's way, their eyes wide and their hearts thumping wildly as animals and bankers, Jesus and priests scurry about. "Zeal for your house will consume me" (John 2:17) they will say, recalling the words of the psalmist and thinking of Jesus. Surely Jesus' zeal for God's house will consume them too.

"'Take these things out of here!'" Jesus shouts. "'Stop making my Father's house a marketplace!'" (John 2:16). The religious leaders charge him, demanding explanation and credentials. He cryptically explains, "'Destroy this temple, and in three days I will raise it up'" (John 2:19). No one knows then that he means the temple of his body.

The other Gospels tell this story later, after the Triumphal Entry, not as preamble but as climax. Jesus arrives in Jerusalem to break up the furniture, the trappings of the religious system as it has come to be. "'My house shall be called a house of prayer'; but you are making it a den of robbers" (Matt. 21:13), Jesus scolds. Not just God's house now but *his* house, Jesus' house. Not just trade but thievery.

From our safe distance we may smile, even laugh, at how Jesus goes after the religious professionals in the Temple. It can make for smug and fiery preaching for those who want to tear into the church as it often is—materialistic and self-serving, institutional and legalistic—as opposed to how we think it should be. It is more difficult and important to see that Jesus comes after us in the temple of our own hearts to find that we have let thieves set up shop and do their daily work. Our minds and souls are full of passions and prejudice, envy and pride, lust and despairing. With our complicity we have allowed those emotions and attitudes to rob us of true intimacy with God. We need cleansing because we take the clean currency of the gospel and exchange it for pennies on the dollar.

The scouring Jesus offers terrifies and thrills. We want our souls to be clean and our prayers as well. But we fear we are not prepared to lose what must be driven from our hearts, our dear and familiar idols. We are caught, sure that one way or the other—with Jesus at the hands of the religious leaders who brook no dissent or at the hands of Jesus himself who suffers no fools—we are about to die.

Tuesday: The Time Has Come

Passover: one of the major festivals that all Jews are expected to attend and the kind of party non-Jews want as well. No surprise then that Greeks come to the festival, either faithful Jews living in another land or Gentiles on hand for the camaraderie or commerce. Some of these Greeks approach Philip, one of Jesus' disciples, and ask him to arrange an audience for them with Jesus.

Philip tells Andrew, and together they go and speak to Jesus, who seems to hear in his disciples' words something more significant than their report of a routine conversation with tourists.

"The hour has come for the Son of Man to be glorified," Jesus states. "Very truly, I tell you, unless a grain of wheat falls into the earth and dies, it remains just a single grain; but if it dies, it bears much fruit. Those who love their life lose it, and those who hate their life in this world will keep it for eternal life. Whoever serves me must follow me, and where I am, there will my servant be also" (John 12:23-26).

It is a terrifying and sudden word. Only two days before, outside the city on the Mount of Olives, things seemed to have been going well. Now, death hangs in the air like an eagle ready to dive, talons bared. Jesus appears ready to bare his neck, give himself over to this fate. "Now my soul is troubled. And what should I say—'Father, save me from this hour'? No, it is for this reason that I have come to this hour" (John 12:27).

But it is not for this hour that the disciples have come, though surely their souls are troubled as well. Will they have to give themselves up too?

When Lazarus fell ill, his sisters summoned Jesus to Lazarus's sickbed in Bethany. Jesus tarries two days before setting out. In that time Lazarus dies and is buried. Still a ways off, Jesus tells the disciples that he is going to awaken Lazarus—to raise him. Thomas imagines that the religious leaders will not stand idly by if Jesus proves to be such a healer. The life of Lazarus will prove the death of Jesus, and Thomas can see it coming. "Let us also go," he says, mustering the other disciples, "that we may die with him" (John 11:16). Perhaps he thinks they will die right then and there in Bethany. His timing is off, but his prescience proves true enough.

Tuesday in Holy Week is the Lenten form of Epiphany. As the Gentiles came to Jesus and proclaimed his identity by virtue of his birth, the Greeks who come signal the fulfillment of that identity—his destiny by virtue of his death.

Wednesday: The Anointing at Bethany

During his time of wilderness trial, Jesus refused the crown the devil offered him. He also refused the populist enthronements offered him after feeding the multitudes and as he entered the holy city of Jerusalem. However, he accepts the scandalous coronation that Mary offers him when she anoints his feet with pure nard, an expensive perfume. Then she wipes his feet with her hair.

Mary's behavior shocks those at the dinner table. No proper woman would let her hair down in public. Her sacrifice also surprises. She may have worked years to acquire this nard for the time of her own death, her own embalming. The disciples do not know what to say, how to react. Only silence and the fragrance of the nard fills the house.

Then Judas Iscariot grows indignant, sputters his angry words to no one in particular. "Why was this perfume not sold?" (John 12:5). The words sound hollow as he speaks them. The Gospel of John notes that Judas is a thief who pilfers from the common purse.

Maybe Mary's devotion embarrasses Judas. How *inappropriate* when Jesus had so clearly told the young man, "Sell your possessions, and give the money to the poor" (Matt. 19:21). Perhaps Judas fears a reprimand and wants to appear as if *he* at least understands. Or maybe he wants to ensure that Jesus' demands of the young man and of him are required for everyone. Judas speaks aloud what all of them are thinking.

"Leave her alone," Jesus says. A different reprimand. "She bought it so that she might keep it for the day of my burial" (John 12:7). Jesus will not live long, but the memory of what she has done will.

After the anointing Judas goes to the authorities and makes a deal to deliver Jesus into their hands. Why does he do that, and why then? The Gospels of Luke and John say that the devil made him do it: that Satan puts it into Judas's heart to conspire with the authorities to destroy Jesus.

Or does something else draw Judas? As Mary anoints Jesus' feet, he speaks of his death. If Judas is not merely a thief and betrayer but a disciple still, he does not want Jesus to die. Perhaps he believes that if he delivers Jesus into the hands of the authorities—into protective custody—then the Passover would give everyone time to cool down. So the next night after supper, Judas meets the soldiers and goes to the Garden of Gethsemane to hand Jesus over.

Whatever Judas dreams might happen becomes a nightmare soon enough. Judas returns the money and tries to undo the deal. He may have hanged himself because he feared that neither Jesus nor the others would understand his hopes and what he had tried to do.

Maundy Thursday: The Foot Washing, Gethsemane, the Trials

The Foot Washing

The Last Supper forces Jesus' friends to face their fears—their fear of intimacy and their fear of separation. We fear both things too, I believe—in our relationship with God and in our relationships with each other.

On Thursday evening Jesus changes the command he gave his disciples when asked about the greatest commandment. At that time Jesus replied, "'You shall love the Lord your God with all your heart, and with all your soul, and with all your mind.' This is the greatest and first commandment. And a second is like it: 'You shall love your neighbor as yourself'" (Matt. 22:37-39). The first command is clear and absolute, unalterable and unchanging. But the second provides a loophole—wiggle room if we do not love ourselves. So at dinner Jesus tightens the loop, closes the hole: "I give you a new commandment, that you love one another. Just as I have loved you, you also should love one another" (John 13:34).

The disciples and Jesus have gathered together one last time. If it is a Seder meal, as many believe, it is unlike any they have ever attended. The elements remain the same: the lamb and the cups of wine, the bread and *charosis*,[1] the bitter herbs and the story of Moses, the plagues and the lamb, God's mighty hand and outstretched arm—the focus of every Seder meal.

Jesus as host, leads them through the ritual meal. But as he does he redefines the Passover story in terms of himself. "The bread is not just matzah, unleavened to recall the haste of the liberated slaves—it is my body, given for you, a sacrifice for your freedom. The wine is not simply a sign of God's provision and life given from the earth—it is my blood, poured out for you and for many, a sign of provision given from my heart" (Luke 22:19 and following, AP).

And then Jesus washes their feet. He kneels before those who have knelt before him. He fills a bowl with water, takes their feet into his hands and bathes them as if in baptism. One by one he washes their feet—as scandalous a devotion as Mary's anointing of him had been. Peter first refuses—not because his feet aren't dirty but because Jesus is their Lord, their teacher, the Holy One of God. This amazing intimacy mortifies Peter. "Lord, are you going to wash my feet?" (John 13:6), he growls, as if to say, "It is I who should wash your feet, and yet you wash mine?"

"Unless I wash you, you have no share with me" (John 13:8), Jesus says. He washes away Peter's protests and misunderstanding with grace.

∞

Maundy Thursday is Command Thursday, the day of Jesus' mandate that we obey his loophole-closing command and follow his example. "Do you know what I have done to you?" he asks the disciples when he has once again taken his seat. "You call me Teacher and Lord—and you are right, for that is what I am. So if I, your Lord and Teacher, have washed your feet, you also ought to wash one another's feet. For I have set you an example, that you also should do as I have done to you" (John 13:12-15).

Every Maundy Thursday I schedule a foot washing, but many of the faithful church members I serve cannot bring their feet to this service, their lack of ease an echo of Peter's. Many fear the intimacy, I think— touching and being touched in a way most of us have not experienced since we bathed our babies or were bathed ourselves. Many also fear the separation, what comes after the service, knowing that day by day most of us so remain distant from one another, so alone in our heart of hearts, that we can only momentarily love each other as Jesus commands. Almost better not to feel it at all than to feel it and feel it gone.

In the foot-washing service, members of the congregation and I gather around water and the word, twenty-five chairs in a circle and a bowl with a small pedestal in its center. Warm water forms a circle in the bowl. I kneel before my congregants one by one, members of the church and others, some of them friends. I take a bare or sometimes stockinged foot into my hand. I place it on the pedestal and with cupped hands ladle water onto it. I look into the eyes of the ones before whom I kneel, whether they can look at me or not. And often they cannot. This sharing, this tenderness, can cut deeply, creating an even deeper impending separation.

I speak of God's love, of Jesus' call, of the grace that is ours as spiritual friends. Tears sometimes come, gasps, for love of God and one another, for fear of losing that love, losing this moment now that we have come to it. We fear opening our closed hearts and lives to others; yet we fear the loneliness if we do not. Who knows what we fear more?

Gethsemane

After the meal and the foot washing, Jesus and the disciples make their way to Gethsemane, a garden, a place of refuge and prayer. Jesus leaves his drowsy disciples, goes off by himself about a stone's throw, and prays to his Father in heaven, begs God for the sake of his hallowed name to let his kingdom come and God's will be done. But please, God, not this way. Jesus prays that God will deliver him from this evil, that the bread he receives the next day will not be the bread of suffering but the bread of heaven. The Gospel writers want us to know that our own agonized prayers are not without precedent: that Jesus prayed as we have, in fear and finally surrender. "Not my will but yours be done" (Luke 22:42).

Sometimes we too find strength to surrender to God's will. And in surrender comes victory.

The Trials

When Pilate hears the crowds shout that Jesus has "claimed to be the Son of God" (John 19:7), John tells us that "he was more afraid" (19:8), implying that the powerful Roman official has been afraid from the start.

Herod also fears, though he tries to cover it with political pretense, threats, and farce. He hopes "to see [Jesus] perform some sign" (Luke 23:8). Herod has been fearful since first hearing of Jesus, thinking that John, whom he had beheaded, has returned from the dead.

Herod: a bully, a surprising enemy to Jesus as a fellow Jew. If Herod does not want Jesus dead, he at least wants Jesus out of his sight. Pilate is more judicious, a manager attempting damage control to protect his own position. For fear of the supposed insurrectionist, Pilate tries to release Jesus. Then, for fear of the crowds, he consents to Jesus' death.

The authorities fear the Romans, the crowds, and Jesus. They fear losing their living and way of life; they fear the Temple might be destroyed. Better to kill one man, they say, than to have everyone die for him. And the disciples have fled in fear of what will happen to Jesus and of what could happen to them. His disciples have deserted him except for Peter who trails behind to see what will become of Jesus. Jesus seems fearless, resigned, and serene.

Good Friday: The Flogging, the Way of Sorrows, the Crucifixion

The Flogging

Why does Pilate have Jesus scourged, parade him around the Praetorium in a purple robe and a crown of thorns? To humiliate him? To appease the crowd's blood fever?

Many of the condemned prisoners did not survive the beating. Hardened soldiers used leather flagellums studded with scrap metal, bone fragments, and stones to peel flesh off the unfortunate's back. Those who survived, if they had strength and sense and senses left to feel anything at all, were surely sorry to have done so.

The soldiers savage Jesus' dignity. They dress him for display, prop him up, a ragged caricature, this "king." Perhaps it occurs to Pilate that the sight of Jesus—ravaged as he was by the hated occupiers, might finally elicit some sympathy on the part of the crowds. He has tried to release Jesus twice and nothing has worked. He finds no crime in Jesus, nothing deserving death. Can Jesus' near death satisfy the mob, forge some identification between the crowd and Jesus on account of their common enemy, the Romans?

Nothing works. Pilate knows that Jesus is right—that he, Pilate, the powerful Roman governor, has no power at all.

The Way of Sorrows

John tells us that Jesus carries his own cross to the place called The Skull. It is hard to imagine that he has back or blood or strength enough after the flogging to carry so much as his own weight down the Way of Sorrows. But John may be speaking theologically as much as historically, saying that Jesus has strength enough to shoulder the sins of the world as well as his own burdens. For his part, Luke tells us that Jesus has help—a soldier compels Simon of Cyrene to complete Jesus' journey to Golgotha.

At spear point, or threat of it, Simon of Cyrene takes Jesus' cross on his shoulder. Simon may have been an unwilling disciple, but that is what disciples do: They find themselves compelled, one way or the other, to carry Jesus' cross to wherever Jesus will give his life. They do so every time they carry their own cross to where Jesus bids them come and die.

The Crucifixion

Jesus hangs between heaven and earth, so much food for the birds. A euphemism for one crucified was "crow bait," and a person might remain on the cross, suspended and naked, for days if the individual was strong enough, struggling to the last for breath to pray for death. It was a ghastly and terrifying spectacle for those with stomach enough to look.

Ghastlier still was when the soldiers decided to end the suffering by breaking the legs of those on the crosses. No longer able to push up to unburden the lungs and draw air, the condemned suffocated quickly.

Jesus does not last so long as that. When the soldiers come to break his legs, he is already dead. The scourging, the loss of blood and hope, break him before the soldiers can administer that last, undignified work on his legs. Surely his surrender has something to do with it: He does not fight death, does not fight for his life. He prays for those who abuse him, blesses those who curse him, forgives those who pierce him, and then he dies. He lives only a few hours, his weakness and strength perfectly joined.

Jesus' company at the last are two criminals flanking him left and right, one at each side in his ironic glory. One derides him, "Are you not the Messiah? Save yourself and us!" (Luke 23:39).

Jesus cannot grant the man's request. Jesus cannot come down, cannot save himself or the malefactor in the way the man demands. Jesus cannot answer the man's tortured prayer. And like Jesus' night in the garden, just the night before and yet so long ago, after his anguished petition, there is only silence and heartbreak. This cup of suffering and death will not pass from any of them.

The other criminal's fear and faith differs. He chides his fellow criminal—"Do you not fear God?" (Luke 23:40), he barks. "We indeed have been condemned justly, for we are getting what we deserve for our deeds, but this man has done nothing wrong" (Luke 23:41). And then, looking to Jesus, he says, "Jesus, remember me when you come into your kingdom" (Luke 23:42).

"Today you will be with me in Paradise" (Luke 23:43), Jesus replies.

This moment resembles no other in the history of the world. Some people have suggested that were they able to be one character in all the New Testament, they would choose to be the "good" criminal who shares in Jesus' last earthly conversation and dies with him.[2] If Jesus died *for* both of those crucified with him, indeed for all those on Golgotha's hillside that day, he died *with* the one who blessed him in his agony.

We too suffer justly for our sins. We fear admitting it, confessing it. We fight against the unavoidable truth that we too are powerless. We see ourselves as isolated and perceive that only we experience separation as we pray our agonized prayers. We are afraid we don't understand, or that we do. We are scared to be alone, scared to be with others. We fear both intimacy and separation. We sometimes believe that being with Jesus only makes following him harder because we find ourselves surrounded by unloving people to love and unmerciful people to forgive. But intimacy, fellowship, shared suffering, come to us if we follow. Where Jesus is, there we are too.

∞

During Holy Week I encourage the members of our church to wear a cross—not like the ones with which we bejewel our fashions but something more stark, large, obvious. Most people wear crosses as an accent not as a symbol of Jesus' suffering.

I invite us to make a different kind of statement, a sign of our absolute devotion at least for these last days of Lent. We drape Jesus' suffering around our necks, an outward and visible sign of an inward and spiritual determination to love whom he loves and serve whom he serves, to follow where he leads and die with him too, should it come to that. We pledge ourselves to Jesus, vowing to give what he asks of us even if that means our lives.

We put on the crosses routinely in these days, but we do not wear them casually. Day by day we try to recall the full significance of this small act, and Holy Week by Holy Week the meaning becomes clearer. We keep his death ever before us and pledge our own. We wear our crosses and make our sacrifices that our lives may become cruciform.

We stretch out our arms to the world. It can be a fearful posture, unfailingly uncomfortable, to shape ourselves after the pattern of a cross. We have to work at it, exercise, build the strength, and quell the anguish. No one wants to die. But to save our life or keep it pristine is to lose it altogether, and that kind of cowardice proves a death more frightening still.

We take up our crosses daily, surrender ourselves to what may come from following Jesus, knowing that to die without him is death indeed. And day by day Jesus chooses to bring his cross to where we are, to be with us.

Jesus' presence gives us strength to live his life, to die our death. His presence does not palliate our pain or alter our circumstance, nor does our surrender. But his presence with us, if we are mindful of it, can make even the most fearful of moments, the most barren of wildernesses, the harshest of crosses a place of conversation and intimacy, a place of friendship with Jesus.

Affirmation: Jesus comes as Suffering Servant.

Confession: We are afraid of his suffering and afraid of our own for his sake.

Discipleship Task: To comprehend the message of his suffering and death as central rather than accidental to his mission and to follow Jesus by moving from fear to surrender.

Advent

Christmas

Epiphany

Lent

Holy Week

Easter [Middle English *estre*, from Old English *astre*; akin to Old High German *starun* (plural) Easter, Old English *ast* east] **:** a feast that commemorates Christ's resurrection and is observed with variations of date due to different calendars on the first Sunday after the paschal full moon

Pentecost

Trinity

Ordinary Time

Reign of Christ

6

From Skepticism to Belief

EASTER DAY AND SEASON

Long before the postmodernists vanquished the Enlightenment chimera of unlensed seeing and ungrounded truth, [Flannery] O'Connor knew her faith to be the basis of her vision. "It is popular," she observed, "to believe that in order to see clearly one must believe nothing." The true order, as she discerned, is the other way around.

—RALPH C. WOOD

Remember how he told you . . . ?" (Luke 24:6).
That is what the bedazzling messengers ask the bedazzled women—Mary Magdalene, Joanna, and Mary the mother of James, and some other women besides. The women are doing their duty, going through the motions, coming to the tomb to embalm their friend, barely thinking and never thinking to hope. There is nothing *to* hope. Not yet.

The women come to the tomb, navigating their way by the first glimmers of dawn. They have come with burial spices, expecting to see nothing other than death, to smell nothing other than stench, to feel nothing other than a fresh wave of grief when they get to the spot where he lies entombed.

Suddenly the light of angels flashes before them, and a new fear frightens them. Two men dressed in dazzling white fill the empty darkness with light. "Remember how he told you . . . ?" ask the messengers. But how can the women remember while holding such grief in their hearts, such a light in their eyes? Why would they want to? It hurts too much, remembering all that their friend, their teacher, their Lord had been through. Grief buries recollection.

Did they remember? Did they believe? In resurrection? At all? Of course they believe in resurrection—at least Martha believes, she the one person Jesus specifically asks that day in Bethany. She believes in a resurrection: that her brother will rise on the last day (John 11:24). That one belief sets her and whoever believes it apart from the Sadducees who believed nothing of the sort. But if the other women, including those who come that morning to the tomb and even the men who follow Jesus also believe in resurrection, perhaps like Martha in Bethany they believe it only in a general way: a "last day" when all the righteous would rise again: reunion and vindication, in the future, all at once. Nothing in their experience or learning has prepared them to think of now or this. And even if Martha and the rest of them after that day in Bethany have come to believe that Jesus *is* the resurrection and the life, how can they have as yet understood or believed that Jesus is himself resurrected and alive?

"Do you not remember?" The question pounds in the women's temples; they search their memories for something Jesus has said that allows them to make sense of this light, these cloths, and the empty tomb. For a long moment Jesus' words of hope or promise seem as buried as their friend. Then all at once something vague begins to take shape, Jesus' words that the angels wanted them to remember, from way back in Galilee: "The Son of Man must be handed over to sinners, and be crucified, and on the third day *rise again*" (Luke 24:7, emphasis added).

Yes, of course, *now* they remember how Jesus said there would be betrayal and suffering and death, but that death would not have the final word. "I am the resurrection and the life" (John 11:25).

Is *this* what he was telling them? That he *himself* would rise again? Is that what he meant?

Who could believe such a thing? No wonder the rest of the disciples do not believe the news when the women tell them what they have seen and heard.

The Crucifixion proved centrifugal for those who loved Jesus. The force of his death shatters them, distances them, drives them away from one another—geographically and otherwise. With all that has happened, they no longer trust one another entirely and perhaps not at all, for promises to Jesus have been made and broken. Protestations of allegiance have evaporated by courtyard fires. Friends have betrayed one another into the hands of merciless people, and fear grips them all. Now they experience doubt, wariness, skepticism.

The women return early on the first day of the week, telling of an empty tomb. At least two disciples go to check out the women's story.[1] They agree the tomb is empty, but that is all they agree on. The women report seeing angels; Mary Magdalene has seen the Lord himself, but the other disciples consider it an idle tale, a rumor, wishful thinking.

"Do you not remember?" the women ask the men, full now with both memory and understanding, but the men do not believe them. Maybe they can't let themselves see beyond the obvious, the tangible. They are fishermen, tax collectors—practical men used to holding in their hands dead fish and cold coins and hard truth. They trade in realities, tendered in common sense, require proof of things. Until they see Jesus with their own eyes, touch him with their own hands, they will not, cannot believe. *Would that it were true*, they think. *I wish it were. But this is the real world. Things like that do not happen.*

∞

On Easter evening, the disciples gather in the upper room; only Thomas is absent. Jesus appears to the rest of them, blesses them and breathes on them, and in that moment they believe what Mary has been telling them since first light. When the disciples tell Thomas that Jesus lives, the disciple expresses skepticism. "Unless I see for myself," he said, "unless I can touch the wounds, unless Jesus himself proves it to me, I will not believe" (John 20:25, AP).

The next week all the disciples gather. Jesus appears and goes toward Thomas, imploring him to see, touch, believe! Jesus says, "Do not doubt but believe" (John 20:27). And Thomas does.

Thomas is the twin of us all. We say the words, but sometimes wink as we do. We do not always believe all of what we are saying and we do not always believe that if it is true, it makes any difference in the real world.

Nothing in our experience, in our world, prepares us for this announcement of Resurrection. But Jesus comes, shows himself both wounded and alive in his word, in the sacraments, in the peace that passes understanding. Rather than anger he extends the invitation to know beyond the verifiable facts, to trust beyond our reasonable doubts, to live beyond the strictures and ravages of time. "Do not doubt but believe."

∞

Easter by Easter in my part of the world, believers get up while the sun is still beyond the eastern horizon to stand shivering with sleepy-eyed friends in the chill of a church cemetery, new candles in hand. Preachers and texts and sometimes even trumpets prompt us to memory and proclamation. "Remember how he told you . . . " a white-robed someone will say, an angel or maybe the preacher. "Christ is risen!"

"Christ is risen indeed!" we the people respond with quavering voices. We do remember, and we want to believe.

With scriptures and hymns, music and flame, we gather ourselves and our voices to the ancient choruses and recite while it is still mostly dark the heart of our faith: how Jesus "was crucified, dead and buried," but on "the third day he rose from the dead." On these thirteen words hang the whole of Christian history, the hopes of all the faithful, the future of the entire world.

Death is not the final word for any of us, for the world itself. That is what we say, what we sing and preach—and we really want to believe it, though sometimes we say and sing with our fingers crossed. We stand in the cemetery after all, and no one has yet come up out of the grave.

We are practical people, real world people, where cancer often proves stronger than our prayers. Sometimes there are reprieves and curings, and we bandy the word *miracle* about, but the miracles are rare. Our loved ones will die. We will die.

It may be an idle tale, an opiate, this message of the Resurrection. Still we want to believe it. We gradually realize that we do not know as much as we flatter ourselves to think. Far more is going on in the world than even the sharpest of young eyes can take in, and by grace older, dimmer eyes see that our only hope for life and death is founded in God, that God's goodness is stronger than the power of death.

So we stand in the cemetery as dawn kisses the headstones. Moment by moment the blushing granite markers reveal names carved deep into the stone of men, women, children. The young and the old who died sudden, tragic death or long, lingering death surround us. As the sun continues to rise, we begin to sing and remember and proclaim and believe that death cannot have the last word. It must not and will not, and that is worth believing this morning and every other.

We remember. We believe. Most of us first approach the story with our intellect—how can it be true? Dead is dead. Sunday by Sunday, Easter by Easter, and death by precious death, we come with the women at first light of dawn and find that in our hearts we begin to trust in what should be true, what ought to be true.

Yes, we believe in what we have not yet seen, what cannot yet be proven. Lord, help our unbelief. We confess that we are skeptics and disciples, but disciples more than skeptics because we rise to proclaim what we have not experienced, not in its fullness. We gather to sing and provoke one another to believe and remember that Jesus is alive again and that we, though mortal as he, shall one day share his immortality.

Together we hear again the curious stories of the women and the angels and the empty tomb. Our bodies shiver; our voices break. If it is *true*, all that the women tell Jesus' followers then and now—that the tomb is empty and there are angels afoot—then that supplies ample reason for our cemeteries and churches to be full Easter Sunday by Easter Sunday.

If, on the other hand, the tomb is not empty, then our faith and our preaching, our worship and our hearts surely are. Paul said it all:

> If Christ has not been raised, then our proclamation has been in
> vain and your faith has been in vain. We are even found to be
> misrepresenting God, because we testified of God that he raised
> Christ—whom he did not raise if it is true that the dead are not
> raised. For if the dead are not raised, then Christ has not been
> raised. If Christ has not been raised, your faith is futile and you
> are still in your sins. Then those also who have died in Christ
> have perished. If for this life only we have hoped in Christ, we
> are of all people most to be pitied. (1 Cor. 15:14-19)

The last sentence of that text always frightens me a little: "If for this life
only we have hoped in Christ, we are of all people most to be pitied." Paul
put all his eggs, as William Sloane Coffin once suggested, in one Easter
basket.

If Jesus has not been raised, those of us who follow him, who name
him and claim him as Lord, are of all people the most deluded. We have
staked our lives and future on a lie, have trusted our souls to absurdity,
have hoped in what is not true and will die wretched, hopeless deaths.

Pity us if Christ has not been raised.

But what if Christ has been raised? If mourning has broken, who then
shall we pity?

If I had been Jesus and I had been raised from the dead, I think I might
have paid an early Easter morning visit to Herod or Pilate. To Annas or
Caiaphas. To the centurion with the flagellum or the other ones with the
hammers and spears. I may have asked for my robe back first, just to see
the look on their faces. Then I might have gone to see my disciples and to
ask why they were surprised. Weren't they listening?

Of course, that is not what happened, not what Jesus did. Jesus had
prayed from the cross, "Father, forgive them; they do not know what they
are doing" (Luke 23:34), and after the Resurrection he practices what he
has prayed. He forgives Thomas who doubts. He forgives Peter who denied
him and ran away.

No surprise then that the forgiven disciples preach the Resurrection itself as a kind of forgiveness. "You acted in ignorance" (Acts 3:17), Peter tells those gathered in Jerusalem for Pentecost. "Repent therefore, and turn to God so that your sins may be wiped out, so that times of refreshing may come from the presence of the Lord, and that he may send the Messiah appointed for you, that is, Jesus" (Acts 3:19-20).

If Christ be not raised, the "real world" is as lost as it appears to be. But if Christ is raised, we are of all people most blessed. We will not fear sickness or death or grieve hopelessly when our loved ones die. We will find a peace that passes understanding and a community of faith that helps make peace in the world. We will face each day with strength and hope, a serenity not based on mere circumstance. We will know the bankruptcy of power for power's sake, of beauty for seduction's sake, of money for self-determination's sake. We will trade with a different currency—humility, service, vulnerability.

We will not fear though heaven and earth should shake, for God alone is eternal and the Resurrection proves it. We will forgive even those who abuse us, pray for those who malign us, share the hope of the Resurrection even with those who consider it an idle tale, wishful thinking. We will remember all Jesus has said, all Jesus has done, and we will say and do likewise till we see him as he is, till we are like him at last. We will believe what we have heard.

Affirmation: Jesus comes as resurrected Lord.

Confession: We are skeptical as to the meaning or import of Resurrection.

Discipleship Task: To hear again the message of the women and angels and to follow Jesus by moving from skepticism to belief.

Advent

Christmas

Epiphany

Lent

Holy Week

Easter

Pentecost [Middle English, from Old English *pentecosten*, from Late Latin *pentecoste*, from Greek *pent kost* , literally, fiftieth day, from *pent kostos* fiftieth, from *pent konta* fifty, from *penta-* + *-konta* (akin to Latin *viginti* twenty)] **1:** *Shabuoth* [Hebrew *sh bh ' th*, literally, weeks]: a Jewish holiday observed on the sixth and seventh of Sivan in commemoration of the revelation of the Ten Commandments at Mt. Sinai — called also *Pentecost* **2:** a Christian feast on the seventh Sunday after Easter commemorating the descent of the Holy Spirit on the apostles — called also *Whitsunday*

Trinity

Ordinary Time

Reign of Christ

7

From Waiting to Witness

PENTECOST

An important aspect of [prayer] . . . has been described as "attentive waiting." I think it's also a fair description of the writing process. Once, when I was asked, "What is the main thing a poet does?" I was inspired to answer, "We wait." A spark is struck; an event inscribed with a message—this is important, pay attention—and a poet scatters a few words like seeds in a notebook. Months or even years later, those words bear fruit.

—Kathleen Norris

Pentecost does not, as it is sometimes portrayed, begin with noise— the rush as of a violent wind, the clash of overlapping languages, or even the crackle of tongues as of fire. Pentecost came to all of that, but it does not begin there.

It begins instead in silence.

The power of Pentecost does not reside in the preaching of Peter or the witnessing done by the other disciples or even human words at all, though there will be power in all that. The power of Pentecost comes in the disciples' waiting and prayer.

The initial movement of Pentecost is not the coming of the Holy Spirit but rather the going, the Ascension, of Jesus. For a moment his disciples stand there, chins in the air and hearts in their throat, looking up into the sky, to the cloud where Jesus has vanished. Who can blame them? More than once over the last few weeks Jesus has disappeared, leaving them alone, only to rejoin them later. First he was taken from them forcefully—crucified, dead, and buried—and then he was alive, miraculously with his disciples again, back in their barricaded upper room. Over and over he disappears mysteriously only to startle and sometimes terrify them by reappearing once more.

Easter afternoon, incognito with two of his disciples—suddenly Jesus becomes known to them in the breaking of bread. But then as quickly as they have eyes open enough to see him, he leaves them.

Later that night, all of the disciples gather in Jerusalem to share their stories of how they have seen Jesus—and suddenly he is with them, to their delight and wonder.

Early one morning, some time later, Jesus comes to the shore of Galilee's sea where a few of the disciples are fishing. The erstwhile and feckless fishermen are still in the boat after a long, tiring night of hauling empty nets from the water, when suddenly, at Jesus' word, they have more fish than they can haul in. By the time they get back to shore, Jesus has made breakfast.

Luke tells us that after Easter Jesus "presented himself alive to [the disciples] by many convincing proofs" (Acts 1:3). Some of them need convincing, for when the disciples meet the resurrected Christ on a hillside in Galilee, many believe and worship, but "some doubted" (Matt. 28:17). Sadly, Luke does relate the details of those convincing proofs. But we know that for forty days Jesus appeared here and there, now and then, sometimes passing through walls and sometimes eating fish, showing his scars, giving the disciples instruction, breathing his breath like peace onto them.

The disciples who believe surely begin to look over their shoulders, glance out the corners of their eyes, listen for the first soft rustlings of

Jesus speaks, and suddenly the man can hear and speak plainly. He is no longer silent in what has seemed to him a silent world; by the gift of God he has power to speak.

The miracle depicts Pentecost. Jesus promises that the Spirit will come and touch the disciples to help them hear and remember all that he said and did, to make them strong to preach all they have seen and known. And so they wait, pray for themselves and their friends that the Spirit will work just such a miracle as that.

And at Pentecost the Holy Spirit does.

∞

Another Sunday down. . . . how many more to go? I ask myself this question some Sundays even before I finish shaking hands. And then, as I walk down the center aisle to gather my things, the self-interrogation intensifies. Did I say today what needed saying? Did I speak the gospel? Did I do justice to the text, to the human condition? Did I preach both the need for repentance and the gift of forgiveness?

And this: If what I just preached were my last sermon, would it be a fitting end for my ministry? Would I be content for that to be my last word on the matter of God's way with the world and with us?

In some ways the first few moments after morning worship are a sweet, placid relief. The week's study and prayer, whether lots of it or little, have found some kind of expression. Even before preaching I have taught a church school class—my faith twice delivered to the saints. Now I can sit down, rest my voice, ice my knee. There are 166 hours before I have to do it all again. Only 166—but 166!

In other ways the first few moments after morning worship are the hardest of the week. I think back over the morning and invariably wish I had taken a couple of more hours for silence—to study a bit more, to read another chapter or two, to pray harder. Maybe if I had written a couple of more drafts, sharpened my similes and polished my metaphors, the sermon would have been better, more effective and winsome.

Most Sundays I walk back down the aisle and shake my head grimly, knowing in my heart of hearts that yet again I did not say all I might have, did not preach either bravely or persuasively enough, did not do justice either to the text or its Lord. So please, God, give me at least one more chance to do it right, to make this next Sunday's effort a fitting "last" one should it come to that.

Next Sunday's sermon, if there is to be one, begins with this silence, this understanding that I have neither the power nor the knowledge to be the kind of witness I am called to be. All of our witness begins in the awareness that we cannot do all of what needs to be done, cannot prove our faith, cannot save the world or its needy children. We must admit that we who pray for the conversion of the world are ourselves in constant need of conversion.

"Not many of you should become teachers" (Jas. 3:1). That verse is branded on my brain. I find myself "judged with greater strictness." My hands always feel cold after I preach and teach—most likely cold with fear of teaching incorrectly or preaching insufficiently, of leading God's people astray.

I need the touch of Jesus before I can begin to offer Jesus to others. There must be silence before there is speech, humble waiting before there is bold witness.

All of us who would witness begin with the confession that we are powerless. Without Jesus, without his touch, without the coming of the Holy Spirit to fire our work, we are sound and fury signifying nothing.

But always that bleak sense of failure and inadequacy, the awareness of another missed opportunity dissipates into a warm awareness of God's prevailing mercy and grace. Jesus had no illusions about the disciples, and we must have no illusions about ourselves. Those of us who name the Name and claim his ministry do so fully aware that we cannot in our own power demonstrate him alive to those who will not believe, cannot offer convincing proof other than ourselves, our common life and work—and those shot through with pride and prejudice. Our lives and witness evidence many gaps, gaping holes. But God has called us, and I believe God is prepared to fill with the Spirit what we lack—if we but wait.

If we do not, if we rush to our work—just go and do—we go naked, unclothed with God's promise and presence. But if we wait, speak when spoken to, tell only what we are given to remember and know, go and do as commanded, we may find we are indeed witnesses in spite of ourselves.

∞

"Of course we are weak," admitted Ghislain Lafont, a French Benedictine who was lecturing a group of younger monks, "unable to cope. But if we can maintain faith, hope and charity, it will radiate somehow. And people who come to us may find in us what we can no longer see in ourselves."[1]

By the time I make it to my office, I bask in the humble awareness that my last sermon, whenever it is, is not *the* last sermon. However many Sundays I have left, God has *all* of them left, and whatever I do not say will get said sometime by someone. It is not my gospel, after all. God will continue preaching, filling in gaps, long after I stop. God *won't* stop till everyone hears at last and believes.

Cold hands? Yes, but a warm heart too. Strangely warmed. I *love* Sunday afternoons.

Affirmation: Jesus sends the empowering and vocalizing Spirit.

Confession: We are eager to speak and reluctant to wait, so our words and our witness avail nothing.

Discipleship Task: To wait and pray for the power God offers us and then to follow Jesus by moving from waiting to witness, from prayer to ministry, from silence to speech.

Advent

Christmas

Epiphany

Lent

Holy Week

Easter

Pentecost

Trinity [Middle English *trinite*, from Anglo-French *trinité*, from Late Latin *trinitat-*, *trinitas* state of being threefold, from Latin *trinus* three-fold] **1:** the unity of Father, Son, and Holy Spirit as three persons in one Godhead according to Christian dogma **3:** the Sunday after Whitsunday observed as a feast in honor of the Trinity

Ordinary Time

Reign of Christ

8

From Familiarity to Mystery

TRINITY SUNDAY

I remember a visit to the ruins of the Fountains Abbey in Yorkshire, when, as we walked from one part of the site to the other, a friend read the relevant text from the official guide at each point. When we reached the ruins of the Chapter House, the text was as follows: "Here the monks gathered every Sunday to hear a sermon from the Abbot, except on Trinity Sunday, owing to the difficulty of the subject."

—LESLIE NEWBIGIN

"Safe?" said Mr. Beaver. "Don't you hear what Mrs. Beaver tells you? Who said anything about safe? 'Course he isn't safe. But he's good. He's the King, I tell you."

—C. S. LEWIS

I still remember walking home from school and stepping through the back door of the house to observe that a remarkable transformation had occurred since that morning. In our back den, the hub and hive of all things in our family, the furniture had been moved out and replaced by a great wooden frame—a couple of sawhorses and long side beams that must have been five or six feet long. White fabric stretched across the frame, a kind of sandwich, really, with a layer of linen on top and another beneath, separated by a padding of cotton. It was a quilting rack, of course.

I still remember the way my pulse quickened. A quilting rack in the den meant my grandmother's sisters were there. Memie, my grandmother, lived to be 104 and a week. My favorite of the sisters was the oldest one, Nanny, an elegant and funny woman. Cokie, the youngest, looked and acted the oldest. She had the sourest expression and grunted with every step. But Cokie—we sometimes called her Pokey because she moved so slowly—made the best blackberry jam cakes in the history of the world.

The cakes came out of the oven, and Cokie would slather them with a sugary icing. There was *nothing* pokey about the way my family members went for our forks and dug in, sometimes without even slicing the cake first. We just ate it whole, right off the plate. Nanny and Memie tried in vain to duplicate Cokie's recipe. Mom tried to duplicate *their* recipe, but it was never the same. The sisters and nieces think Cokie held out on them, did not include a crucial ingredient and took the secret to her grave.

Whatever intrigue characterized the kitchen, none of it occurred at the quilting rack. I loved to watch the three of them, sitting here or there, stitching awhile, sometimes talking among themselves, sometimes silent except for Cokie's grunting. One of them, or two of them, or all three as if on cue would move their chairs to start working somewhere else. I found it a mysterious dance, and when they performed it they too grew mysterious.

The three sisters looked different somehow when they quilted; their faces and postures changed with the work. They almost glowed. And sometimes they glowered too. Then I knew to keep my distance and hold my tongue—at least till they looked up or stopped for the day. Or maybe their quilting and conversation changed me. I stood transfixed, watching in awe as a beautiful creation took shape.

I could never tell exactly what the sisters were doing; sometimes it looked as if they stitched in the same place over and over again. Day after day I would come in from school to find the three of them at their work. I would check their progress, and for the longest time it looked like random stuff, haphazard patterns.

But there came a day, there always came a day, when I would return from school and see that what had seemed random had been more purposeful than I could have imagined, that their movements and stitching here and there were not haphazard at all but part of a plan and design that my elementary-age eyes could not recognize.

The women's craft lay beyond me. *They* knew what they were doing. I simply watched. *They* stitched a quilt that would warm me on a cold winter's night, and into that quilt they poured their years of experience and skill and love.

∞

On Trinity Sunday Christians proclaim the fullness of God—Father, Son, Holy Spirit in an inner life and relationship, eternally One and yet eternally distinct, one God in three persons, and three personal ways of knowing and experiencing the One eternal God—as God has *gradually* been revealed to us. This doctrine of ours is a mystery; few scriptures point to it directly. And as Augustine noted, we cannot know a true mystery unless it is revealed; and even after it is known, it cannot be explained. The Trinity constitutes such a mystery: known by revelation; evidenced in creation, in salvation, and in abiding presence.

In the beginning, when only darkness and chaos and void existed, God said, "Let there be light," and there was light. Only later did we realize that the Word by which God created the world was the eternal Word, the Word that would become flesh and dwell among us. John tells us, "In the beginning was the Word, and the Word was with God, and the Word was God. . . . All things came into being through him, and without him not one thing came into being" (John 1:1, 3).

Only later did we realize that in Creation, as the Word was being spoken, God's Spirit was moving on the face of the deep, that God's Spirit came upon the prophets so they would proclaim God's will, that God's Spirit came upon a virgin who conceived and bore a Son who was the Word made flesh.

God comes among us, stands apart from us, fills our lungs with breath. But as close as God might be in any given moment, God remains far beyond us. Though we have seen Jesus' face and known his salvation in the sacraments and worship, he remains a mystery. Though the divine image is imprinted on us, we are still strangers; if we know God, we still do not know God whole.

For the Hebrews, the holiness of God's name precluded its being spoken. When Jesus taught us to pray, he allowed us more familiar access to the Father. But familiarity should not lead us to presumption, for God is Spirit and we are dust. God is eternal and we are locked in time. We may know a language or two, but God understands every utterance made, speaks in all the languages of earth and heaven besides. We may move the earth and feel ourselves mighty, but God made the earth and all of us from it.

God invites us to converse; Jesus calls us friends; the Holy Spirit speaks to our spirits to tell us that we are God's children. But we dare not presume too much familiarity—though we, like Jesus' contemporaries, often do.

As Jesus goes about his work in Galilee, many people think they know him. "Is not this Joseph's son?" (Luke 4:22) they would remark, or words to that effect. "Is not this the carpenter, the son of Mary?" (Mark 6:3). The latter serves as a dismissive statement, though we do not always hear it as such—one never called a Jewish male by his mother's name unless uncertainty, real or imagined, existed about the father's identity. The former is a benediction, but in both cases the speakers assume that "we know who this is." One way or the other, the crowds think, *He is one of us.*

One day Jesus teaches near the Sea of Galilee. So many people have come to hear him, hungry for the word of God, that they crowd him almost into the water. Jesus gets into Simon's boat and has Simon put out a little ways from shore so he can finish the lesson. When Jesus finishes teaching, he instructs Simon to put out into the deep water and let down his net for a catch. Simon has fished all night and caught nothing. Before Jesus' arrival, Simon is washing his nets, through for the day. But he does as Jesus asks, and sure enough his nets fill with so many fish that Simon calls for help to bring them in. When Simon and his friends get the fish into the boat, the boat begins to sink.

Everyone is amazed, but Simon is amazed *and* afraid! He falls at Jesus' feet and says, "'Go away from me, Lord, for I am a sinful man!'" (Luke 5:8). He knows Jesus well enough to know he does not know him at all. He knows himself well enough to be frightened in the Lord's presence.

Simon differs from many of us who, like the crowds in Capernaum or Nazareth, imagine that Jesus is just like us—that he thinks as we do and values what we do.

Trinity Sunday reminds us that for all our presumed familiarity with God, God is much more than we can manage. We know God, but we do not know God at all—God's ways are not our ways nor God's thoughts our thoughts. God's Spirit bears witness with our spirits that we are the children of God, but children do not always know their parents in their full personhood. They may know some of what their parents do and certainly how their parents care for them, but they do not often know all of who their parents are. Not for long years, anyway, not without much conversation and life experience of their own.

Mystery suffuses the familiarity. Familiarity gives way to mystery; and as we grow, who can tell which quality prevails or is more precious? I often tell my students that we walk in the surf and what splashes on us is all ocean. But it is not *all the ocean*. We love the ocean, but we dare not presume we have mastered its depths or fail to remember that mystery resides there—even danger.

We, like children, are left to wonder as to the fullness, the depth, the person of God. We know what God does, some of it; we have experienced God's love and care. We have been splashed with baptismal waters, and we sense the living near the edge of God's fullness. But it takes years for us to begin to know who God is. Our elementary eyes have only gradually come to see what God has been doing all along. Only gradually have our eyes come to see who God has been all along.

∞

On July 8, 1741, in the church at Enfield, Connecticut, a thirty-eight-year-old Puritan preacher by the name of Jonathan Edwards delivered one of the famous sermons of all time, "Sinners in the Hands of an Angry God." Even nonbelievers have heard of this sermon:

> The bow of God's wrath is bent, and the arrow made ready on the string, and justice bends the arrow at your heart, and strains the bow, and it is nothing but the mere pleasure of God, and that of an angry God, without any promise or obligation at all, that keeps the arrow one moment from being made drunk with your blood. . . . God holds you over the pit of hell, much as one holds a spider, or some loathsome insect over the fire.[1]

Edwards, a guest preacher in Enfield that day, had people weeping and wailing, passing out right and left. The pastor kept trying to interrupt Edwards, asking, "But what of mercy? Is there no mercy?"

For Edwards that day, maybe not. Maybe there was no mercy. The God Edwards presented had no concern about the tragic consequences of sin—what we might call our plight and predicament—but only with protecting and preserving a particular kind of almighty honor: God's wrath, a justified and justifiable outrage because of willful disobedience and original sin. God's one emotion: an implaccable and irredeemable anger.

Edwards lived a long time ago. Most modern people in many modern places have shifted completely away from his theology. The pendulum has swung. If Edwards and others like him made God too foreign, too different and "other," in the long days since many preachers have persuaded us that we know who God is: our familiar friend, always warm and close, so very much like us.

Most Sunday mornings the sermons offer all mercy and no judgment. All blessing and no demand. We no longer imagine God in terrible or capricious terms. That change in perception is a good thing and biblically founded, except sometimes we go to the other extreme. We can imagine God as domesticated, always accepting and understanding, always glad to see us, never displeased or demanding. We think of God as our copilot, our rabbit's foot, our personal assistant, or our fire insurance. We see God as our help but not as our Lord; our last resort but not our first love. God is a safety net, a secret weapon, a sanctioner, no matter what we set out to do. God so loves us just the way we are. We experience no mystery, no danger, no call to change or need for repentance.

In the Puritan days we witness sinners in the hands of a too mysterious and capricious God. In these latter days we see a too familiar God in the hands of self-satisfied sinners, capriciously remade in our own image and likeness.

Trinity Sunday and the doctrine it proclaims remind us that God is as near as our breath but not so familiar as to warrant presumption. God lies beyond time and space but not so mysterious as to be inaccessible or terrifying. We are sinful people. When faced with the goodness and power of Jesus, we instinctively and rightly beg him to depart. But Jesus says, "Do not be afraid; from now on you will be catching people" (Luke 5:10).

In Jesus' call to Simon, in his call to us, he issues the invitation to intimacy but also abiding mystery. Fear gives way to faith, but Simon will never know Jesus completely. When he thinks he does, presumes to challenge him, he will find himself in the hands of an angry Lord.

God is not at our disposal, but rather we are at God's. There is always more to God, both mercy and demand, than we ever completely see or imagine. For that reason Eugene Peterson has said that the Trinity is actually the most practical Christian doctrine of all and the simplest—this gradually revealed awareness of God's fullness. Father, Son, and Holy Spirit remind us that there is always more of God than we can know, always more of God than we can explain, always more of God than we can show. The Trinity says God is much bigger than we imagine. God is more powerful than we sometimes want to believe or remember, but in remembering it we find great comfort.

∞

William James, the famous American philosopher, used the term *the More* to refer to the Mystery beyond space and time in which all of us live and move and have our being, whether we acknowledge that Mystery or not. Most of the time most of us don't. Instead we live and move and have our being in the familiar and manageable surface of things. We live little question to little question—What's for supper? Who won the game?

Now and then, we realize upon what thin ice we tread, how easily the surface can crack and give way. A child gets sick or finds herself in some kind of trouble. A parent dies or betrays us one way or the other. A spouse no longer exhibits interest, and what we had imagined as our lasting worth and value is cast aside as rubbish. Big business proves as heartless as big government; big government proves as selfish and inept as big business. War does not beget peace, only more war, and the church . . . the church? Let's just say that the church does not always practice what it preaches, does not always preach as it should.

Age is relentless, and so is the devil. Disease comes or disillusionment. We stroll through our days till the moment comes that we stumble or fall, when we scratch the surface of our awareness or it gets ripped wide open. Something or someone, some person or situation, breaks our heart and ruptures our security, and suddenly we find ourselves in the depths, asking ourselves the harder, colder questions of life and faith, of death and hope, of meaning.

We go deeper. We *have* to go deeper to survive, to find the More that lies beyond a given space or a given time, to find food that can satisfy us beyond our immediate hungers or craving, to find that truth to hold like an anchor when the storm sweeps away all lesser opinions. And when we do, we find the Savior not only above us but below us, in us and around us. He is the More who lovingly desires to meet every "I."

∞

I cannot explain the Trinity, this most foundational of our doctrines. All the explanations we have been taught or teach our children are inadequate and even idolatrous: water, ice, steam; apple, peel, core; father, husband, brother. None of that helps. But if those images help us begin to see that more is going on in the world than we can possibly domesticate and more to God than we can ever imagine or manage, more than we can observe or understand, then the little explanations have done their service.

No one can explain it. I tell the story of my grandmother and her two sisters, and it is not a perfect analogy by any means. But it pleases me to think of the Father, the Son, the Holy Spirit, each of them and all of them together fussing over our world, working here and there, sewing, stitching, unstitching.

It pleases me to believe there is a cake in the oven too, by which I mean that God is preparing a feast for all God's children, and no ingredients are missing. Soon all of us will dig in and wolf down that delicious eternal confection whose recipe continues to elude our best efforts. But there are racks and chairs, conversations and commotion, random movements and haphazard concentrations, and some day soon we will see what the Three were up to all along, what the One was up to while we were doing other things.

One day soon, there will be a world that will keep us all warm and fed and blessed and at peace. *They* know what they are doing, the Father, the Son, and the Holy Spirit. I believe that. Even now they are stitching and restitching sense and light and purpose into the fabric of our world. *They* are crafting something wondrous, pouring all their skill and love into the world, making something lasting just for us.

Affirmation: God is mysterious, triune, *More* than we can imagine.

Confession: We try to keep God small, manageable, and thereby miss or ignore the wonder and the blessing of God's fullness.

Discipleship Task: To move from presumptuous familiarity to humbly embrace the mystery of God who is both beyond us and among us in Jesus.

Advent

Christmas

Epiphany

Lent

Holy Week

Easter

Pentecost

Trinity

Ordinary Time [Corresponds to the Latin term *Tempus per annum* or "time through the year"] : A season of the Christian liturgical calendar comprising two periods—one following Epiphany, the other following Pentecost—which do not fall under the "strong seasons" of Advent, Christmas, Lent, or Easter

Reign of Christ

9

From Boredom to Contentment

ORDINARY TIME

A child kicks its legs rhythmically through excess, not absence, of
life. Because children have abounding vitality, because they are
in spirit fierce and free, therefore they want things repeated and
unchanged. They always say, "Do it again"; and the grown-up
person does it again until he is nearly dead. For grown-up people
are not strong enough to exult in monotony. But perhaps God is
strong enough. . . . It is possible that God says every morning,
"Do it again," to the sun; and every evening, "Do it again," to the
moon. It may not be automatic necessity that makes all daisies
alike: it may be that God makes every daisy separately, but has
never got tired of making them. It may be that He has the eternal
appetite of infancy; for we have sinned and grown old, and our
Father is younger than we.

—G. K. CHESTERTON

Turn your eyes upon Jesus,
look full in his wonderful face,
and the things of earth will grow strangely dim
in the light of his glory and grace.

—HELEN LEMMEL

It has often been said, as Saint Augustine famously put it, "You have made us for yourself, O Lord, and our hearts are restless until they rest in you."[1] All of us contain a God-shaped hole and though we try to fill it with other, lesser things, we find no peace until we fill that hole with God. We cannot outrun the emptiness any more than we can outrun our own shadow, cannot quench our spiritual thirst unless God does the pouring.

Many of us are reminded of this fact time after time. We experience moments when we remember both who and whose we are, when we pledge once again to be and become all God created us to be. Other moments remind us of life's evanescence, the fragility of our own existence and that of the world. We plead with God, pledge ourselves again to God, know that God alone provides eternal refuge and lasting peace. Whether insight or ignorance blind us, we assure ourselves in these singular times that what we need is God's to give.

But in between the big moments come other moments, ordinary times, when we all but forget what we know so well, when the ebb and flow of our days hypnotizes us into spiritual amnesia, rocks us almost to sleep. If we come to again, we discover our discontentment as we look elsewhere for refreshment and nourishment and peace, search in places and look to things that cannot provide them.

We get bored, distracted from the ordinary presence of God. We crave excitement instead, ground-shaking experiences, spiritual or not. Most often the Lord is not in the earthquakes or fire, but we find ourselves turning away from the still small voice until the next significant insight or crisis. Then we search again for Jesus, praying he will fill the God-shaped hole once and forever.

We most often live our spiritual lives by fits and starts. Jesus, however, lives his life with constancy, always looking to us. His determination to seek and to save that which is lost reveals the "us"-shaped hole in the middle of God's heart. God finds no rest until God is at peace with us, and we are at peace with God.

Both we and God lack one thing: each other. While we realize that truth only sometimes, God knows it always and constantly seeks us for both our sakes.

One day a man comes to Jesus asking after eternal life. Maybe he simply means, "How do I get to heaven?" or perhaps, "What will make my life meaningful, real?" Of all the New Testament characters, I believe he resembles us most. We have and still want. We acquire and feel the poorer for it. We fill our lives with many things and yet are barren. The world affords us many distractions, so many diversions, endless entertainment, and we remain bored. This man too. Whatever fills his life, he still feels empty. We recognize in him that all-too-familiar hole in each of us.

For Jesus' part, he loves the man and invites him to be a follower and a friend. In Jesus' call we discern the other and surprising hole, the one in Jesus.

The story ends badly: Both holes remain empty. The man leaves empty and Jesus does too in a way, goes on without him anyway, both of them grieving and traveling their separate ways. The man believes in Jesus, but believing isn't enough. Jesus loves the man, but Jesus' loving him doesn't guarantee their relationship or intimacy. Jesus will continue to seek and to save those who are lost. The man will continue looking for what he has rejected.

We don't know the man's name. If his answer to Jesus had differed, we might know him as well as Simon or Andrew, James or John. We might remember him as the rich disciple who gave it all up for the gospel, a foreshadowing of Saint Francis who gave up the wealth and prestige of his father's legacy in favor of living in a cave and preaching to the birds. All of these incarnated the words of Psalm 19:9-10:

> The ordinances of the LORD are true
>> and righteous altogether.
> More to be desired are they than gold,
>> even much fine gold.

The Hebrew word translated "desire" is the same word as the one translated "covet" in the Ten Commandments. You shall not covet another's stuff, but you shall desire the Lord God. We come wired to desire and we will, in fact, want. But sometimes we don't acknowledge our wiring, don't know what we want. God does, though, and just as Jesus desires the rich man to desire him more than he does his gold, God wants us to want God more than anything. God desires to give us God's self more than anything.

The man does not want Jesus that much, however, and turns away. He will not pay this price, even for eternal life. The irony is this: Jesus states that the young man has too much; he holds too many things in his hands to take hold of Jesus.

Jesus doesn't fuss. He doesn't yell or scream or threaten the man with hell if he refuses Jesus' call. There is just this sense of loss. For both of them. Whatever they might have done together, however each might have enriched the other, it is all for naught as the man goes his way and Jesus continues his, never to meet again. Except, of course, they do. And I wonder what that reunion looked like.

Maybe the man said, "I am sorry, Jesus. I wanted to and couldn't. Forgive me. I am dust." And Jesus would reply, "Of course, I forgive you. I loved you then; I love you now. I died for you. Still, I wish you had come with me that day." The man probably noted, "Me too."

Or maybe the man says this: "You know, I couldn't sleep for weeks thinking about what you said. I kept hearing your words over and over again in my mind. Later I did what you said. I sold what I had and gave it to the poor. I tried to find you after that, catch up, but I never could. I did my best to follow at a distance though."

And Jesus would have said, "'Well done, good and trustworthy slave; you have been trustworthy in a few things [late but trustworthy], I will put you in charge of many things; enter into the joy of your master" (Matt. 25:21).

∞

The church calendar, start to finish, rightly focuses on the big events, the major moments in the story of Jesus—his coming and birth; the visit of the wise men; his suffering, death, and resurrection; his appearances to the disciples until his ascension; and then his sending of the Holy Spirit.

What happens in between the big times is as workaday as the word *ordinary* connotes. What I find most interesting about Jesus during these in-between times is that each day looks like every other day in Jesus' life, and he never seems bored. Frustrated sometimes, tired and angry too. But he never seems distracted.

It is hard to follow Jesus' example in this way. Jesus stays constant, content, seldom resting or stopping. He is God-focused, sure of his mission, unwavering. His ministry is, as Eugene Peterson put it in his book by the same title, a "long obedience in the same direction," whether in the big moments or the other moments. He keeps doing what he was sent to do, interruptions and detours notwithstanding.

One time Jesus receives a summons to the home of Jairus, whose daughter lies near death; time is of the essence. A woman who has been bleeding for twelve years interrupts Jesus, touches him. He knows it, turns, and asks, "Who touched me?"—a silly question in a way, for many people pressed in on him. "Who touched me?" and the woman fesses up. Her action could have incurred Jesus' anger, just as he might have been angry at the leper that morning after all the healings in Capernaum or at the people following him and clamoring after him. He has no time to himself or with his disciples. Yet he has compassion on all of these, takes time to heal, to teach, to feed—true to his mission, interruptions or no.

∞

One of the stories we tell during Ordinary Time is the only miracle recorded by all four evangelists—the feeding of the five thousand. In Matthew Jesus feeds five thousand *men*, which may mean that altogether three or four times that many followed Jesus: twenty thousand people maybe. That number is significant because, by the end of John 6, the crowds have all left to go looking, we assume, for someone or something else to fill their empty stomachs. Only the Twelve are left, and Jesus asks if they too want to leave, to go back to their homes and families, their old way of life.

It is Passover, a time to remember how Moses led the people out of Egypt. Jesus looks a little like Moses, only Jesus walks on the water instead of parting the sea. Jesus does not provide the hungry people manna or water from a rock but rather his own flesh and blood. It is Passover, but it is different too.

Jesus is a prophet like Moses but more. He is a king but other than and different from David. His teaching taxes the imagination of the restless, hungry people, for he demands that they think beyond their stomachs. Yes, they are hungry, but they need so much more than bread. He makes a point, teaches a lesson, feeds them less out of compassion and more by way of instruction, trying to show his disciples and the crowds that he himself *is* the provision of God, the meaning and purpose of their lives and of all history beyond the momentary.

"I am the bread of life," Jesus said. "I myself am the manna, but more, other, different, better. The bread the Israelites ate all those generations ago perished as they themselves did in the wilderness. The bread you ate just a while ago—what's in your belly and what's left of it in these baskets—it too perishes, goes stale, feeds the earth or feeds the birds. People who eat *only* this food likewise perish. But if anyone eats my flesh, which is bread indeed, and drinks my blood, which is drink indeed, he or she will never die. I am the *living* bread" (John 6:48-51, AP).

We hear Jesus' words and think of the Eucharist. The people hear his words and aren't sure what to think. "How can this man give us his flesh to eat?" (John 6:52), they whisper. They think literally, physically. He will be their nourishment, their food and drink. He alone can and will fill the empty place, offer them a salvation they cannot yet imagine.

Many turn away, confronted as they are and confounded by this lesson. It remains one of Jesus' hardest teachings: that this one particular man living at this one particular time is God's once-and-ever unique means of eternal salvation; only by coming to *him*, eating and drinking of him, do God's children find the contentment they crave and need.

Many that day have come only for a meal and perhaps a miracle. What they get in addition is a blunt tutorial, and so many circle back and go away. Some days I can understand. Following Jesus does not always satisfy in most of the ways we count satisfaction. We would rather love our stuff and hate our enemies. We would rather live for the day or advance our own purposes. We would rather keep our gold and turn away from Jesus' command and invitation, even if the hole threatens to swallow us.

Following Jesus is hard—hard at all times and harder still in the ordinary moments and times of our lives. It is easier to quit paying attention, to look away, to pretend we don't hear. We find it easier to doze through Jesus' daily sermons than to take him at his word. No wonder, then, that many of his disciples, then and now, though they began to follow him, turn away when the teaching gets rough and look for other instructors and counsel by which to live.

But some know already that the world's wisdom resembles a confection, as airy as mousse. Other teachers do not give us faith, hope, or love enough to shoulder real life or real death. When life kicks us in the shins or breaks our hearts, when we are bored with life as it is and forced to confess how little we can do to improve it, where shall we go, whom should we see about that? Simon Peter knows.

When the disciples have left, Jesus turns to his twelve closest friends and asks them, "Do you also wish to go away?" (John 6:67). Simon Peter asks Jesus a question in turn: "Lord, to whom can we go?" (John 6:68).

Simon Peter's query is more than rhetoric. Before Jesus can say another word, Simon Peter answers his own question for the Teacher and for the Twelve and for the rest of us too: "You have the words of eternal life. We have come to believe and know that you are the Holy One of God" (John 6:68-69).

Affirmation: Jesus comes to us in the ordinary moments of life.

Confession: We are easily bored and so turn back or look elsewhere for fulfillment.

Discipleship Task: To stay with Jesus in the ordinary moments of our lives, to feed on him as our daily bread, to rejoice in his peace as our contentment.

Advent

Christmas

Epiphany

Lent

Holy Week

Easter

Pentecost

Trinity

Ordinary Time

Reign of Christ 1: Reign of Christ Sunday celebrates the all-embracing authority of Christ as Ruler of the cosmos. Officially called the Feast of Our Lord Jesus Christ the King, it is celebrated on the final Sunday of Ordinary Time, the Sunday before Advent

10

From Faith to Sight

REIGN OF CHRIST

Born thy people to deliver, born a child and yet a King
Born to reign in us forever, now thy gracious kingdom bring.
By thine own eternal spirit rule in all our hearts alone;
by thine all sufficient merit, raise us to thy glorious throne.

—CHARLES WESLEY

It seemed to Us that peace could not be more effectually restored
nor fixed upon a firmer basis than through the restoration of the
Empire of Our Lord. We were led in the meantime to indulge the
hope of a brighter future at the sight of a more widespread and
keener interest evinced in Christ and his Church, the one Source of
Salvation, a sign that [people] who had formerly spurned the rule
of our Redeemer and had exiled themselves from his kingdom were
preparing, and even hastening, to return to the duty of obedience.

—POPE PIUS XI

One afternoon when I was in college, I stopped by my father's office, a little room in the basement beside the back stairs of a two-story building—barely large enough for two drawing boards and my father. He had landed there after a tumultuous period in his professional life. Months before he had been in a second-floor suite with four employees and a good engineering business, so good that he had been bought out by a larger firm downtown. He went to work for the new owners, making more and more than he ever had, but the time clock and the strictures of being an employee quickly began to chafe. What had seemed the promised land at last—steady hours and a steady paycheck—soon felt like wilderness and exile, and so he quit the new firm, left his former employees there, and went back to the basement of his old building, alone and with few clients. There I found him that afternoon.

We did not talk about his business; we talked about his soul. Perhaps the peaks and valleys of recent days had left him uncertain, unsure of God's will or purpose in his life. The outward stuff was making my father look inward, to ask whether God existed or cared. My father could not see the way forward.

I will never forget what he asked me, "Have you ever wondered if you really were saved?" The question stunned me. I had given my eight-year-old life to Jesus sitting on Daddy's knee. Surely he had not forgotten. Or was he conducting a test, one last experiment, and if I said yes right away, it might be the end of him, proof positive of his absolute dereliction—God was not with him then and never had been.

Or maybe he was asking me not father to son but preacher to preacher. I was serving a small congregation in Nashville. Suddenly it dawned on me that his true concern was this: After preaching deliverance to the captives, have you ever wondered whether you yourself might be a castaway?

Is it true, after all, what we preach and believe and proclaim? True not only for those who hear it but also for those who preach it? Is this Jesus the One, the One for all so that all may find in this One hope and love and, until we can see, faith? Jews and Gentiles, slave and free, rich and poor, men and women?

Paul wondered the same thing, of course. So did the prophet Elijah, John the Baptist, and John Wesley, founder of the Methodist Church.

∞

Seven hundred years after the time of Isaiah, another prophet appears among the people of Israel, dressed in skins and leather. John appears in the wilderness, and many go to see him for themselves. They have heard of prophets but have never seen one, at least not like John. He preaches repentance and baptism, and many receive baptism at his hands to signal their desire for cleansing. John himself desires cleansing, confesses as much when he sees Jesus wading toward him in the water. He sees more besides: "Look, here is the Lamb of God!" (John 1:35), he says one day to his own disciples, two of whom leave John to follow Jesus.

Fast forward. Now John finds himself in a different kind of wilderness. He is in prison and sends some friends to Jesus to ask a question: "Are you the one who is to come, or are we to wait for another?" (Luke 7:19).

This poignant question introduces a critical moment in the Gospels: the preacher, with his strength for preaching almost gone, is unsure of what he has been preaching all these years. It happens.

So John sends friends to Jesus, the one who takes away the sin of the world, in the hope that Jesus can take away the doubt in his heart. If Jesus is the way, the truth, and the life, then imprisonment and even death at the hands of Herod poses no threat. If Jesus is not all these things, then imprisonment and death at the hands of Herod might bring relief, an end to John's disillusioned hopes.

But how will John know for sure? He cannot judge by what his eyes see because he is in prison and unable to see much of anything. In fact, John can only judge by what his ears hear because his friends and disciples tell him.

Jesus said to them, "Go tell John what *you* see and hear; healing is going on and that should be proof enough. Blind folks get sight and deaf folks get sound and the poor are blessed by the preaching of good news. If you believe me and if you tell what you believe, John will believe you and trust me. His faith will be restored, prison or no, and your faith will be rewarded and everyone will get happy if no one takes offense" (Luke 7:22-23, AP).

John awaits a word from his friends; he will believe if they believe. My father was waiting in his office for a word from me, and he would believe if I believed.

All around us people are waiting. They will believe if we believe, but sometimes we too wait—in prisons of one kind or another, whether of disappointments or regrets or grief, of anger or pride or prejudice. Perhaps it is we who cannot see Jesus right now for whatever reason.

But if our friends tell us that, yes, it is all true, that they can see as they never saw before, can hear things they never heard, then maybe we can trust them and begin to believe again that what we have said and sung and maybe even taught all these years is the truth after all. Not just for some but for all, and if not altogether now then eventually. Eventually.

If we begin to believe again, then those who look to us can begin to believe again, and they will be able to tell their friends in prison that this gospel of Jesus Christ is true.

We do believe. That is what John's disciples told him not long before he died. And that is what I told my father not long before he died. I told him in just the way he had told it so often to me. "Yes, Daddy, you can believe this gospel. You can trust this One. Soon all will be set right. Soon we will all live in the light. Soon there will come a shoot of hope from the dead stump of our hearts. Faith will be sight. Soon, and very soon."

I had believed the good news about Jesus when Dad told it to me, and I believe he believed it or believed it again, when I told him that afternoon. Yes, we can all believe, trust, what we have so often told one another, that Jesus is the Way and the Truth and the Life. He comes to us in our wilderness and keeps coming that we might follow and come to him at last.

∞

It is all one Story, really, the good news of Jesus Christ, the Son of God. Jesus' friends tell us they have seen and heard and that we can believe, can trust, can have faith in this Jesus till we have eyes to see him for ourselves. We will see him—the scriptures' promise is clear—but until we do, we can trust those who have been with him.

The Story Jesus' friends tell us is a great narrative arc looping back on itself, year after year. Start anywhere and eventually you will go everywhere. Open your New Testament to Matthew or Luke, and before you are done, you will have read Mark and John. Come with Jesus to the riverside, and you will go with him to the Sea of Galilee. Follow him into the home of Simon Peter or Simon the leper, and you will soon be a guest in Bethany in the home of Mary and Martha and Lazarus. Go cheering with Jesus to Jerusalem, and you will come weeping with him to Gethsemane—and after that fearfully to the courtyard of Caiaphas, the palace of Pilate, the court of Herod, and the hill called Calvary. Die with him and you will be raised with him; love his appearing and you will see his departing, his ascension but also his return.

Bethlehem's manger, Nazareth's synagogue, Olivet's brow, the garden's tomb, the New Jerusalem—all form one geography, one place where God meets us in Jesus, where heaven meets earth. Begin with the beginning and you will come to the end; begin here at the end, the reign of Christ, and you will come back to the beginning. He came; he is coming. He was promised; he is expected. His birth breaks all time into before and after. His life breaks every pretense and convention. His death breaks down every ethnic hostility, destroys every racial barrier, gathers every people into one people. His judgment scatters, separates, divides. His grace forgives, restores, unites.

It is all one Story, the story of Jesus—but with many episodes, many chapters, many discrete characterizations. He creates the world yet cannot create faith. He heals but is helpless. He gives life and falls victim to murder. He appears after his death but not everyone sees. He is one Jesus, the very One about whom people tell a many-faceted Story.

Invoke any of Jesus' names and eventually you will call him by all of his names, will crown him with many crowns, will pray to him all your prayers, will praise him for all his works.

Among Jesus' many names and appellations are these: the King of kings and Lord of lords. The word *king* rasps in modern ears, as does *lord*. Many moderns consider such terms ciphers of oppression and patriarchy, easy encryptions for crusades and hypocrisy, and they reject Jesus outright if only because Christians call him King and Lord.

Saying Christ is King does not suggest that Jesus resembles other kings who are tyrants or gods, jokers or jesters, anachronisms and impotent potentates.

No, saying that Christ is the King of kings and Lord of lords implies that he is first of all because he is "servant of all" (Mark 9:35). Saying Christ is King recalls how he took his place with sinners and riffraff, ate with outcasts and touched lepers. He came not to be served but to serve.

Saying Christ reigns brings to mind how, when he comes out of the tomb, he does not charge the halls of Pilate or the courts of Herod but instead takes a Sunday afternoon walk with two of his disciples. They have no idea who he is but need to see. It comes as no surprise that when he begins to bless and break the bread, they recognize him.

Jesus always took a lower seat, kneeling to pray, to wash his disciples' feet, to be nailed to a cross. He lived and died to serve, and he lives again for exactly the same reasons—to save and serve his chosen, his children.

To say that Christ is King is to say that his kingdom is not of this world—we cannot take a train there. His kingdom is on the map of every human heart, a destination toward which all God's children journey, lost and detoured though we seem to be. The reign of God comes among those whose hearts turn in the direction of the Land that has been promised, wandering and wayfaring though we sometimes feel we are. Christ is Lord of all who love him and even those who don't; he is King of this world, though his reign seems all but hidden, and he reigns as the King of the world to come.

When peace is made, when repentance is preached and forgiveness experienced, when the hungry are fed and the homeless housed, when the powerful are brought down from their thrones and the meek inherit the earth—here and there, now and then, we begin to see a little of what will one day be everywhere and for always.

Until then, Sunday by Sunday, season by season, year by year, we proclaim this end as our starting point, this faith as the beginning of our sight. This promise provides the premise of our worship, this consummation our invitation to sing, to pray, to receive, and to give: Jesus Christ, the Alpha and the Omega, the first and the last, the once and coming and eternal King.

All we say of Jesus, all we claim about him and for him, all we pledge of ourselves to him draws its meaning from this end. Saint Julian envisioned an end that she described in this way: "And all shall be well. And all shall be well. And all manner of things shall be well." It was, I think, her way of saying Christ is King. Has been, will be, and therefore is. The end of our faith is also its beginning, and its beginnings already prefigure the end: Christ is King.

∞

In 1934, Karl Barth and others of the confessing Church in Germany published the Barmen Declaration, a thunderous proclamation of the primacy of Christ as a denunciation of all this-worldly usurpers and pretenders to his throne. Hitler and the state church that supported his Reich were the primary targets of Barth and his colleagues, but their yes to Jesus was a no to many Christ-pretending leaders.

Nine years before the Barmen Declaration, in 1925, Pope Pius XI inaugurated the Feast of Christ the King (or the Reign of Christ) as a doxological celebration of the same truth. If Barmen's prophetic declaration offered pastoral comfort to those endangered by the Nazis and their court prophets, the priestly feast constituted prophetic liturgy—a diminution of the powers and principalities that war for our allegiance.

Both Barmen and the feast have at their heart this one impulse, to exalt Christ and Christ alone, to shame the lesser powers of earth, to remind all disciples along their various journeys that their first, last, and abiding allegiance belongs to Christ, who pledges his abiding allegiance to us.

∞

A framed picture my son Jacob drew of me when he was about four adorns one wall of my study. My body is a line and my arms another line crossing my body at more or less right angles. My legs are short sticks. I find it surprising that I can stand or keep my balance. My head is a big circle with a crooked smile stretched across one side of my face and a few uneven teeth. I am wearing some kind of hat. At the end of each of my stick arms is a ball (my hands) and each of them sprouts fifteen or seventeen fingers, little lines coming out all sorts of ways. I am tilting to the side a bit. Above the picture are letters—my wife, Jo, told me later how she wrapped her own hand around Jacob's and helped him form the crayon words—"My Dad." It is not the most recognizable or accurate picture ever made of me, but because Jacob drew it with love, it is the most precious.

The church wraps its hands around ours and helps us write our words, for when it comes to drawing our pictures of Jesus, all the various portraits his life and work inspire us to draw, I suspect that even our most objective and studied efforts still look, to his eyes, more or less like that picture in my office. But we keep drawing them, remembering how he is coming toward us in love. Our pictures proclaim our love of him and remind us of his allegiance to us—his forever-and-always promise to be with us, come what may. And we in turn promise to stay with him, come what may, until he comes at last.

We remind ourselves that although all we can sometimes see with our natural eyes are the tyrants, dictators, false prophets, and fearsome pretenders, theirs is not the last word or the lasting power. When we are afraid, when the voices whisper in our ears that we must acquiesce, go along, give the devil his due—in those times especially we remember our stories, draw our pictures, hold fast to our hope, and sing—even with quavering voice,

> This is my Father's world.
> O let me ne'er forget
> that though the wrong seems oft so strong,
> God is the ruler yet.
> This is my Father's world:
> why should my heart be sad?
> The Lord is King; let the heavens ring!
> God reigns; let the earth be glad![1]

Soon light will cleave the dark pall draped over the broken earth and its poor, miserable creatures and the befuddling gloom that smothers the hearts and minds of God's children. The thick clouds of doubt and war that have hidden the heavens and dimmed our vision were stabbed through at Bethlehem, but their complete dissipation is now at hand. We have been waiting a long time.

Until that morning, we sing. Until we see, we believe. Until we know, we tell to all those who are imprisoned that we do believe in God; we do trust in Jesus his Christ who is and who was and who will be, the coming

One and Savior of the world, the once and future King of the universe, blessed be he. His Holy Spirit is among us even now as power and comfort and peace.

That is a Story to tell to the nations, a song to sing in the night, a word to calm the fears and quicken the steps of every journeying disciple, of every pilgrim soul.

Affirmation: Jesus comes to us as the once and future King.

Confession: We do not always see Jesus and so we doubt his reign.

Discipleship Task: To worship and proclaim that Christ is King till we move from faith to sight.

Notes

Introduction: Jesus Calls, Disciples Follow

1. Lauren Winner (lecture, WNCC Order of the Elders, Kanuga Conference Center, Hendersonville, NC, November 13, 2006).

1: Promises in the Dark (Advent)

1. I use *holy* here in the sense of "set apart," not as morally faultless or, as we sometimes incorrectly say, "saintly."

2: God with Us (Christmas)

1. The Greek word is translated among Orthodox and Catholic Christians as "Mother of God," granting special recognition to Mary. The literal rendering is "God-bearer," a designation given by Jesus to everyone who has faith (see Mark 3:34).
2. See, for example, the "Infancy Gospels," in Montague Rhodes James, *The Apocryphal New Testament* (Oxford: The Clarendon Press, 1924–1975), 88–89.
3. For theological and historical reasons, Roman Catholic and Eastern Orthodox Christians maintain that Mary remained a virgin her whole life. Scholars in these traditions rightly note that "firstborn son" does not necessarily imply other sons and that the Greek term for "brother" or "sister" (see Mark 3:34, for example) can be translated "cousin" or even "fellow citizen." Most Protestants are unbothered by the notion of Mary having other children—such as James, the "brother of Jesus," who while not an original member of the Twelve comes to be head of the church in Jerusalem (see Acts 15:13-21).
4. W. H. Auden, "For the Time Being," in *Collected Poems*, ed. Edward Mendelson (New York: Random House, 1976), 280.
5. Ann Weems, *Psalms of Lament* (Louisville, KY: Westminster/John Knox, 1995), xvii; based on Romans 12:5.

3: From an Exclusive to an Inclusive Faith (Epiphany)

1. Emily Dickinson, "Tell all the Truth but tell it slant," http://nongae.gsnu.ac.kr/~songmu/Poetry/TellAllTheTruthButTEllItSlant.htm.

5: From Fear to Surrender (Holy Week)

1. A mixture of apples, raisins, and nuts that recalls the mortar used by Egyptian slaves to build the pyramids. See Pastor Michael Smith and Rabbi Rami Shapiro, *Let Us Break Bread Together: A Passover Haggadah for Christians* (Brewster, MA: Paraclete, 2005), xviii.

2. Simone Weil, in *Waiting for God*, cited in Rueben P. Job and Norman Shawchuck, eds., *A Guide to Prayer for Ministers and Other Servants* (Nashville: The Upper Room, 1983), 114.

6: From Skepticism to Belief (Easter Day and Season)

1. See John 20:8-10. The context implies their belief in Mary's word, not in the fact of the Resurrection.

7: From Waiting to Witness (Pentecost)

1. Cited in Kathleen Norris, *The Cloister Walk* (New York: Riverhead Books, 1996), 363.

8: From Familiarity to Mystery (Trinity Sunday)

1. Edwards's sermon can be found in many places, including http://www.ccel.org/e/edwards/sermons/sinners.html

9: From Boredom to Contentment (Ordinary Time)

1. Saint Augustine, *The Confessions*, book 1, paragraph 1, trans. Maria Boulding, OSB, Vintage Spiritual Classics (New York: Vintage, 1997), 3. Boulding's rendering of Saint Augustine's Latin is, "Our heart is unquiet until it rests in you."

10: From Faith to Sight (Reign of Christ)

1. Maltbie D. Babcock, "This Is My Father's World," 1901.

Leader's Guide

Each session begins with an OPENING, a quote from the book and scripture passage that go along with the season, a series of discussion questions and ways to reflect on each season, and a CLOSING.

How to Use This Guide

Invite participants to read the quote and Bible passage aloud in order to set the context. Ask a volunteer to read the quote that follows the opening prayer and another volunteer to read the Bible passage listed. These readings will provide background for the session.

Each session covers two chapters of the book, so divide the time into two 20–25-minute halves. Clear and reset the altar at the midpoint as the study moves to the next liturgical season.

You will have choices to make. Don't think you have to get through all the REFLECTING options! Pick and choose based on the makeup of the group and what gets people talking.

The study will work best if participants read the chapters before class. Be sure they have a copy of the book. The sessions stand alone; a participant can miss a week, but the scope of the study is a big picture. Attending as many sessions as possible will enhance knowledge and understanding.

Setting the stage with colors and symbols of the seasons will help people learn in new modes and make them feel cared for. If the group members are open to going on a minifield trip, you can check with your pastor or the altar guild to see the parament (stoles and altar cloths) collection in your church or add more symbols.

Discipleship, a key theme of the book, can be a shared experience. Perhaps the study will spur some ideas about how group members will share their discipleship outside this group.

Salvation history is another theme. Steagald connects Bible stories to their precursors. Encourage participants to bring their Bibles, so they can check out the references and expand their study.

Some writing exercises will require paper, pens, and a timer. Study participants are always surprised by how much writing they can do in just a few minutes.

Sacred Days offers a chance to learn about Jesus' life, the life of the church, and the lives of those who read the book. May God bless this rich experience!

Session 1: Introduction

Jesus Calls, Disciples Follow

Materials: Blue, white, red, green, purple cloths that cover a small table, candle, matches

Prepare the space: Spread blue, white, red, green, and purple cloths on a small table in the center of your meeting space. These colors represent the seasons of the church year that you will be studying. Place a candle on the table and light it at the start of your time together.

OPENING

Convener: Lord Jesus Christ, may we ponder the sacred days of the church year, holy seasons that reveal your story to us.

Others: As it was in the beginning, is now, and ever shall be.

"I use the Christian year (the Temporal Cycle, as it is sometimes called) as a map. The seasons of the Christian year—from Advent through the Reign of Christ—constitute the church's traditional telling of the story of Jesus' life and also suggest an implicit itinerary for our journey with him. As we recount Jesus' movements, season to season, we will affirm certain aspects of his life and work. Those affirmations will prompt confession that because we often remain self-focused, as individuals and as a church, we have often failed to go where Jesus goes, to do what Jesus does. But with confession comes the opportunity for repentance and renewed dedication to go wherever Jesus leads" (page 12).

READING SCRIPTURE
Ecclesiastes 3:1-8

REFLECTING

- Does your faith community observe the liturgical year? How do you realize that a new season has arrived at your place of worship? Who takes the responsibility for "dressing" your worship setting? (The Roman Catholic Church began using the colors violet, red, white, black, red, and green to differentiate liturgical seasons during the 1300s. After the Reformation, Lutherans and Anglicans continued to use these colors.) How do the colors set the tone for each Sunday?

- Jesus' disciples seek to journey from a self-centered faith toward a God-centered faith. Do you consider yourself a disciple of Jesus? Why or why not? Where would you place yourself on your discipleship journey of following Jesus?

- What parts of the church year do you value most? least? Why? The title of this book is *Sacred Days*. What parts of your life do you consider sacred? What parts of your faith community's life feel the most sacred to you?

CLOSING

Convener: Jesus, bless us now as we begin this journey with one another and with you.

Others: May we follow you in paths of righteousness and discipleship. Amen.

Session 2: Advent and Christmas

Promises in the Dark: Advent

Materials: Blue cloth, votive candles, matches, words to "O Come, O Come, Emmanuel," white cloth, simple nativity scene

Prepare the space: Spread a blue cloth on the table and place a candle for each participant on the table to signify the season of Advent. Wait to light a candle until the discussion time.

OPENING

Convener: Lord Jesus Christ, may we ponder the sacred days of Advent and Christmas, holy seasons that reveal your story to us.

Others: As it was in the beginning, is now, and ever shall be.

The season of Advent, which begins the fourth Sunday before Christmas Day and ends Christmas Eve, proclaims both grace and judgment, mercy and indictment.

Reading Scripture
Isaiah 11:1-2

Reflecting
- On the first Sunday of Advent, Pastor Steagald tells the children in his church, "We light the candle, and it is like asking God to send us more light" (page 18). Give each participant a chance to light a candle and name the light they hope for in Advent.
- "God comes to us that we might come back to God. God comes near to us in love. It is a long, hard journey on both ends, whether God's trek to us or ours to God" (page 21). Invite someone to read aloud the story about the woman in the bookstore that begins on page 21. What meaning does that story convey to you?
- Why does Steagald begin his book with the story of creation? How does preparing for Jesus by lighting Advent candles connect us to the times of darkness God's people lived through from the beginning?

Sing a verse of the Advent hymn "O Come, O Come, Emmanuel."
Convener: In the beginning, creation was good, then broken.
Others: We too are broken, and we pray for the healing that Jesus alone can bring. Amen.

God With Us: Christmas

Prepare the space: Remove the Advent symbols and blue cloth. Replace them with a white cloth and a simple nativity scene to represent the Christmas season.

"Christmas, as we often observe it, blinds us to anything but Christmas itself. Its properties are those of an icon—a window opened to grant our prayers access to God. By grace God grants us, if we will, to see through the celebration itself to God's love of the world" (pages 30–31).

READING SCRIPTURE
Luke 2:6-7

REFLECTING
- Chapter 2, "God With Us," includes stories of Zechariah's silence, Mary and Elizabeth's prophecies, and Joseph's risk. Share with a person next to you how the discipleship of one of these characters spoke to you.
- "'Glory to God in the highest heaven, and on earth peace'" (Luke 2:14) is not a clichéd refrain for the children's angel chorus on pageant night but the full measure of God's will for the world and its children. Jesus, born to save the world, comes as healer for all God's wounded children" (page 31). If God's salvation filled the empty places in your community this Christmas night, what would be different?
- On page 31 the author describes a special service held at his church during the Christmas season for those who mourn and grieve various losses. How did reading about this service deepen your understanding of the Christmas story? What would it take to host a similar service in your community?
- At the bottom of page 30 and moving on to page 31, the author introduces the idea of Christmas as a window into which we gaze to see God's grace. Spend some moments together in silence looking at the nativity scene.

CLOSING
Convener: Jesus' birth confirms God's love for a broken world.
Others: We celebrate God's love for the world by making space in our lives to receive Jesus in all the ways he comes to us. Amen.

Session 3: Epiphany and Lent

From an Exclusive to an Inclusive Faith: Epiphany

Materials: White cloth, candle, matches, cut-out stars (optional), purple cloth, cross, paper and pens for writing

Prepare the space: Place a white cloth and a candle on the table at the center of your group to signify the season of Epiphany. Cut out stars to strew across the table. Light the candle at the start of the session.

OPENING

Convener: Lord Jesus Christ, may we ponder the sacred days of Epiphany and Lent, holy seasons that reveal your story to us.

Others: As it was in the beginning, is now, and ever shall be.

"While the full scope of God's plan, along with the identity of the One who will accomplish it, has been largely hidden until now, Epiphany unveils, proclaims, celebrates God's gift to all people" (page 42).

READING SCRIPTURE

Matthew 2:1-12

REFLECTING

- "Epiphany offers the wondering world comparable loving testimony, tells us of God's plan from the beginning of the world to its end: to choose all of us, to unite all fractured humanity into one family, one people" (page 40). Epiphany's message is prophetic, as it warns those who dare narrow the scope of God's redeeming love. The message is pastoral too, for those who for one reason or the other have felt on the other side of erstwhile lines. How many fractures within humanity can you count in this moment? Which Epiphany message resonates with you—the prophetic call or the pastoral call? Why?
- "The foolish wise men follow a star and, like the frightened shepherds who saw the glory of the Lord shining all around them, they make their way to the One who will bring light in the darkness, peace in the chaos, oasis in the wilderness, and company along the way" (page 43). What gifts did the magi bring *you* by making their journey to find Jesus?
- In chapter 3, we not only follow the magi to Jesus, we follow Jesus to his baptism, to the wilderness, and to the seashore where he calls his first disciples. Steagald describes one of the signs of our discipleship: "We will be known by a new company and a borderless geography and a fresh way of looking at people and things" (page 50). In what

ways does your faith community reflect shifts from exclusive to inclusive faith?

- Some churches hang up a star to to commemorate the journey that the magi undertook to follow the star and find Jesus. How has your faith given you a strong sense of following Jesus? What do you fear about finding Jesus?

Convener: Jesus is not only the King of the Jews but Savior of the world.
Others: May we proclaim the good news that Jesus came for us all. Amen.

From Entitlement to Selflessness: Lent

Prepare the space: Remove the white cloth and stars of Epiphany. Spread a purple cloth and place a cross on the table to signify Lent.

"Lent begins on Ash Wednesday, a little over six and one-half weeks before Easter. It is a season apart, a tithe of the year as some have called it, a time to give ourselves, join ourselves more closely to Jesus. We remember that the one born King of the Jews and Savior of the world will suffer to do God's will in the world, and that those who follow him must suffer with him and die with him, if it comes to that" (page 57).

READING SCRIPTURE
Joel 2:12-13

REFLECTING

- Steagald writes that the ashes we receive on our foreheads on Ash Wednesday remind us that our lives on earth are not permanent, and we must live our lives accordingly. How did Jesus' first followers "live their lives accordingly"?
- "Lent demands we acknowledge both that we need straightening and that we cannot straighten ourselves" (page 58). How does this image of Lent connect to your preoccupations of late? What needs straightening in your life that you've tried to straighten yourself?
- "When we take something away from our lives and give it to God, we create space. We rely, in one more way, on God's sufficiency" (page 59). Talk about what you have given up (or taken up) for Lent in the past. What separates your faith community from God? Spend some time in silence as a group, confessing what separates you from God.

- Write for two minutes each about your answers to these Lenten questions: Who is the Son of Man? What are the costs of discipleship? Who do you say that Jesus is?
- "Not everyone wants a suffering Messiah" (page 61). Who do you know who views Jesus from a different perspective than you? What has been your experience of trying to talk to each other about Jesus?

CLOSING

Convener: Jesus' ministry proved dangerous and far from our desires for Jesus to ensure our success.

Others: May we move with Jesus from entitlement to selflessness. Amen

Session 4: Holy Week and Easter

From Fear to Surrender: Holy Week

Materials: Purple cloth, cross, candle, matches, white cloth, plant or flowers, paper and pens for writing

Prepare the space: Spread a purple cloth and place a cross on a table in the center to signify Holy Week. Light a candle before the session begins.

OPENING

Convener: Lord Jesus Christ, may we ponder the sacred days of Holy Week and Easter, holy seasons that reveal your story to us.

Others: As it was in the beginning, is now, and ever shall be.

"Holy Week resembles the rest of Lent, only more intense. Every day brings a story of conflict. Every day a drama of redemption plays out. The fear that has accompanied the disciples along the way heightens. Everyone is afraid—the authorities, the disciples, and perhaps even Jesus.

"Jesus 'set his face to go to Jerusalem' (Luke 9:51), knowing full well what awaits him there. He moves past his fear to surrender—'not my will, but yours be done' (Luke 22:42)—and he expects that his disciples will too" (page 65).

READING SCRIPTURE
John 13:34-35

REFLECTING

- *Palm Sunday:* Jesus "allows the crowds, his friends and enemies, to make of him what they will—a king, a criminal, a victim, or even a sacrifice. He still does" (page 68). What impressions would visitors get of Jesus' story if they visited your church on Palm Sunday?
- *Maundy Thursday:* What does Maundy mean? What does Jesus' mandate for us to love one another have to do with this chapter's title—"From Fear to Surrender"? Steagald surmises that we fear our separation from one another. How do you think we try to hide our need to be together?
- *Good Friday:* "Jesus prayed as we have, in fear and finally surrender. 'Not my will but yours be done'" (Luke 22:42), (page 74). How do you imagine God would answer that prayer for you? Who around you glimpses God's will for your life?
- "That is what disciples do: They find themselves compelled, one way or the other, to carry Jesus' cross to wherever Jesus will give his life. They do so every time they carry their own cross to where Jesus bids them come and die" (page 75). What opportunities do you have to share in another's suffering? What did those times teach you?
- Read aloud the passage on page 77 about wearing crosses during Holy Week. Share a story about a cross that you own.

Convener: Jesus comes as Suffering Servant, but we fear his suffering and our suffering for his sake.

Others: May we move from fear to surrender. Amen.

From Skepticism to Belief: Easter

Prepare the space: Remove the purple cloth and the cross that represented Holy Week. Spread a white cloth in its place, and add the cross and a plant or a bouquet of flowers to represent the new life of Easter. Relight the candle.

"Yes, of course, *now* they remember how Jesus said there would be betrayal and suffering and death, but that death would not have the final word. 'I am the resurrection and the life' (John 11:25).

"Is *this* what he was telling them? That he *himself* would rise again? Is that what he meant? Who could believe such a thing?" (page 82).

Reading Scripture
Luke 24:28-35

Reflecting
- Steagald begins this chapter by talking about Jesus' followers remembering that Jesus had told them about his coming death and resurrection. What are some of your earliest memories of hearing about Jesus? Did you hear about his life and death?
- "They [the disciples] are fishermen, tax collectors—practical men used to holding in their hands dead fish and cold coins and hard truth. They trade in realities, tendered in common sense, require proof of things. Until they see Jesus with their own eyes, touch him with their own hands, they will not, cannot believe" (page 83). What's your favorite Jesus appearance episode? How much of your enthusiasm for retelling the Easter story comes in recounting the disciples' reaction to the news?
- What do you wish you could express to your neighbors about new life in Jesus Christ as you head off to worship on Easter morning?
- *If Christ is raised.* . . . Use this phrase as a writing prompt, and write for two minutes about how you would complete it. Read your responses to one another.

Closing
Convener: Jesus comes as resurrected Lord. How can we understand this miracle?
Others: May we listen ever more faithfully to the women and the angels. Amen.

Session 5: Pentecost and Trinity Sunday
From Waiting to Witness: Pentecost

Materials: Red cloth, red rose petals (optional), candle, matches, white cloth, spool of thread and needle (optional)
Prepare the space: Spread a red cloth on the table in the center. Some European churches sprinkle red rose petals from the church balcony on

Pentecost, in case you want to add another touch to the table. Light a candle before your session begins.

OPENING

Convener: Lord Jesus Christ, may we ponder the sacred days of Pentecost and Trinity Sunday as they reveal your story to us.
Others: As it was in the beginning, is now, and ever shall be.

"Pentecost does not, as it is sometimes portrayed, begin with noise—the rush as of a violent wind, the clash of overlapping languages, or even the crackle of tongues as of fire. Pentecost came to all of that, but it does not begin there.

"It begins instead in silence" (page 89).

READING SCRIPTURE
Acts 1:1-5

REFLECTING

- What do you appreciate about this focus on the silence rather than the din of Pentecost?
- The power of Pentecost resides in the disciples' waiting and prayer. If you wait, speak when spoken to, tell only what you are given to remember and know, go and do as you have been commanded, you may find that you are indeed a witness in spite of yourself. What are you waiting for?
- Steagald shares a story about what it's like to be the preacher on Sundays (page 93). What surprised you about this story? What did it reveal to you about pastors and about Pentecost?
- "'Of course we are weak,' admitted Ghislain Lafont, a French Benedictine who was lecturing a group of younger monks, 'unable to cope. But if we can maintain faith, hope and charity, it will radiate somehow'" (page 95). Spend time in the group naming the faith, hope, and charity you see in one another.

Convener: Jesus sends the empowering Spirit, but we find it hard to wait and listen.
Others: May we wait and pray for the power God offers us, and then follow Jesus by moving from waiting to witness. Amen.

From Familiarity to Mystery: Trinity Sunday

Prepare the space: Remove the red cloth and petals that connote Pentecost, and spread a white cloth on the table to symbolize Trinity Sunday. You could add a needle and thread as a reminder of Steagald's story about quilting. Relight the candle.

"On Trinity Sunday Christians proclaim the fullness of God—Father, Son, Holy Spirit in an inner life and relationship, eternally One and yet eternally distinct, one God in three persons, and three personal ways of knowing and experiencing the One eternal God—as God has *gradually* been revealed to us" (page 99).

Reading Scripture
2 Corinthians 13:13

Reflecting
- Steagald compares his grandmother and great aunts sewing quilts to the distinct but connected teamwork of the Holy Trinity. How did this comparision stimulate your thinking about the Trinity? Where do you see teamwork in the reign of God?
- Though we have seen Jesus' face and known his salvation in the sacraments and worship, he is a mystery still. We know God, but we do not know God at all. Ask participants to find a partner and talk about these two questions: What do you believe about God? What do you wonder about God?
- "God is not at our disposal, but rather we are at God's" (page 99). What does this idea mean to you in light of the author's words about the danger of domesticating God? Where do you see God being underestimated? What would have to be true for the pendulum to swing to another view of God?
- "*They* know what they are doing, the Father, the Son, and the Holy Spirit. I believe that. Even now they are stitching and restitching sense and light and purpose into the fabric of our world" (page 105). How does the author bear witness of his belief to readers?
- How do you try to keep God small?

CLOSING

Convener: God is more than we can imagine. We try to keep God small, and then we miss the blessing of God's fullness.

Others: May we humbly embrace the mystery of God, who is both beyond us and among us in Jesus. Amen.

Session 6: Ordinary Time and Reign of Christ

From Boredom to Contentment: Ordinary Time

Materials: Green cloth, leaves or plants (optional), candle, matches, paper and pens for writing, white cloth

Prepare the space: Spread a green cloth on the table to symbolize Ordinary Time. It is known as a growing season, so you could add leaves and plants. Light a candle before the session begins.

OPENING

Convener: Lord Jesus Christ, may we ponder the sacred days of Ordinary Time and the Reign of Christ Sunday as they reveal your story to us.

Others: As it was in the beginning, is now, and ever shall be.

"The church calendar, start to finish, rightly focuses on the big events, the major moments in the story of Jesus—his coming and birth; the visit of the wise men; his suffering, death, and resurrection; his appearances to the disciples until his ascension; and then his sending of the Holy Spirit. What happens in between the big times is as workaday as the word *ordinary* connotes" (page 110).

READING SCRIPTURE

Proverbs 3:5

REFLECTING

- Steagald notes Peterson's statement that Jesus' ministry is a "long obedience in the same direction." What stories from Jesus' ministry serve as touchstones in your life? How does your spiritual life shift when you focus on Jesus' obedience rather than your disobedience?

- "Following Jesus is hard—hard at all times and harder still in the ordinary moments and times of our lives" (pages 112–13). What makes discipleship hard for you, ordinary day after ordinary day. Ask group members to add their reasons.
- Talk about gardens. What are the stages of growth for plants? How are the stages of discipleship growth similar?
- "Jesus states that the young man has too much; he holds too many things in his hands to take hold of Jesus" (page 110). Write down the things in your life that you are holding on to. Share them with one another. What things do you share in common that you cling to?
- When in your life have you longed for some ordinary days? How was God with you during that time?

Convener: Jesus comes to us in the ordinary moments of life, but we are easily bored and look elsewhere for fulfillment.

Others: May we stay with Jesus in the ordinary moments of our lives. Amen.

From Faith to Sight: Reign of Christ

Prepare the space: Remove the green cloth and plants that signified Ordinary Time and spread a white cloth in honor of Reign of Christ Sunday. Relight the candle.

"Until then, Sunday by Sunday, season by season, year by year, we proclaim this end as our starting point, this faith as the beginning of our sight. This promise provides the premise of our worship, this consummation our invitation to sing, to pray, to receive, and to give: Jesus Christ, the Alpha and the Omega, the first and the last, the once and coming and eternal King" (page 120).

READING SCRIPTURE
Matthew 11:2-6

REFLECTING
- Ask a group member to read aloud the episode on page 116 about Steagald and his father's question. How does this holy-ground story

ring true with you? How would you answer his father's question: "Have you ever wondered if you really were saved?"

- "Saying that Christ is the King of kings and Lord of lords implies that he is first of all because he is 'servant of all'" (Mark 9:35), (page 119). Which is harder—calling Jesus a king or calling ourselves servants?

- "It is all one Story, really, the good news of Jesus Christ, the Son of God. Jesus' friends tell us they have seen and heard and that we can believe, can trust, can have faith in this Jesus till we have eyes to see him for ourselves. We will see him—the scriptures' promise is clear—but until we do, we can trust those who have been with him" (page 118). How do you listen to stories about Jesus in new ways since you've participated in this study and viewed a bigger picture of the church year and God's whole story of salvation?

- What will you carry with you from the experience of reading and studying *Sacred Days*? What would you like to ask the author? Write about this question for two to three minutes.

- In what ways does the church year seem the same yet different with each passing year?

CLOSING

Convener: Jesus comes to us as the once and future King.

Others: But we do not always see Jesus, and we doubt his reign. May we worship and proclaim that Christ is sovereign till we move from faith to sight. Amen.

About the Author

THOMAS R. (Tom) STEAGALD is the senior pastor of Hawthorne Lane United Methodist Church, Charlotte, North Carolina. An elder in the Western North Carolina Conference of the UMC, Tom is formerly adjunct professor of preaching, worship, and evangelism at Hood Theological Seminary (AME Zion). He is widely published in journals and periodicals (*Circuit Rider*, *The Christian Century*, *Biblical Preaching*), commentaries (*Feasting on the Word*, *Feasting on the Gospels*, *The Abingdon Preaching Annual*), and books (including *Shadows, Darkness, and Dawn* and *A House of Prayer* from Upper Room Books). For three years he blogged weekly for www.goodpreacher.com/. He has also blogged for theolog.org. Tom plays bass in a rock-and-roll oldies band and has two grown children.

CPSIA information can be obtained at www.ICGtesting.com
Printed in the USA
BVOW04s0115080415

394976BV00007B/14/P